Praise for *Ho*

Since time immemorial, the conc_____ _____ _____ _____has been crammed into self-help language, reminding us that we can never be enough and turning what was meant to be a loving relationship with the Trinity into the Christianity Olympics. Jessica gently removes this popular Scripture from its place on the Do-It-Yourself Shelf and flips it on its head, as she says in the introduction, it's the *"fruit of the Spirit*, not the *fruit of trying harder."* I cannot recommend this devotional enough for anyone who desires to go deeply into the Word to discover how God changes you with power and delight.

Erin Moon
Resident Bible scholar on *The Bible Binge* podcast and author of *Memento Mori, Every Broken Thing*, and *O Heavy Lightness*

Many of us want to experience the fruit of the Spirit in our lives but are unsure of what that really means. If you're like me, then you wind up spinning your wheels to cultivate more fruit in your life only to end up exhausted and depleted because we are going about it all wrong. Prepare to be wowed and encouraged as you walk through this forty-day devotional. I'm so thankful for Jessica Thompson's *How God Loves Us*, which points us to Jesus, is immersed in the gospel, and reminds us to walk in the Spirit.

Lindsey A. Holcomb
Coauthor of *God Made All of Me, God Made Me in His Image, Rid of My Disgrace*, and *Is It My Fault?*

Jessica Thompson takes us on a glorious and refreshing tour of love, joy, peace, patience, kindness, goodness, faithfulness, and gentleness—examining how the triune God displays each in His love for us. Thoroughly biblical, packed with good news, and served in perfect proportions, *How God Loves Us* serves the fruit of the Spirit as a feast for the soul.

Eric Schumacher
Pastor, podcaster, coauthor of *Worthy: Celebrating the Value of Women and Jesus & Gender*

Few voices have influenced my understanding of and gratitude for the gospel like Jessica's. What she writes, I read, because I know it will be anchored in what Christ has done *for* us and how His grace *transforms* us. Well, she's done it again in *How God Loves Us*. This devotional frees us *from* striving to produce the fruit of the Spirit in our lives and frees us *to* behold Christ, who perfectly embodied the fruit, and whose Spirit manifests His character *in* us. Jessica reminds us that in beholding Him, by the power of the Holy Spirit, we become more like Him!

JEANNIE CUNNION

Author of *Don't Miss Out: Daring to Believe Life Is Better with the Holy Spirit*

Setting our hearts on God's unwavering character is the only thing that will get us through this age of fracture and disorientation. This book is our blueprint. With clarity, humor, and hard-won wisdom, Jessica Thompson invites us to lay down our striving and simply abide in God's love. What might happen if we truly remembered who God is? A revolution of goodness. A shared hope.

SHANNAN MARTIN

Author of *The Ministry of Ordinary Places* and *Falling Free*

It's so easy to get swept away with this me-me-me culture we live in. As much as we want to focus on God more than ourselves, it's our nature to center our lives, thoughts—even our faith—around "me." If you (like me) are in need of a redirection in your focus—if you (like me) need help setting your gaze on the glory of our God, this book is for you. Jess turns away from a me-centered reading of fruit of the Spirit in order to reveal the goodness of God in each characteristic. You will leave each day's reading with a sweeter sense of who God is and His deep love for you.

KATIE ORR

Author of *Secrets of the Happy Soul* and the FOCUSed15 Bible studies

HOW GOD LOVES US

40 DAYS TO DISCOVERING HIS CHARACTER IN THE FRUIT OF THE SPIRIT

JESSICA THOMPSON

MOODY PUBLISHERS

CHICAGO

Unless otherwise noted, all Scripture quotations are taken from the Christian Standard Bible®, Copyright © 2017 by Holman Bible Publishers. Used by permission. Christian Standard Bible® and CSB® are federally registered trademarks of Holman Bible Publishers.

Scripture quotations marked MSG are taken from THE MESSAGE, copyright © 1993, 2002, 2018 by Eugene H. Peterson. Used by permission of NavPress, represented by Tyndale House Publishers. All rights reserved.

Scripture quotations marked NIV are taken from the Holy Bible, New International Version®, NIV®. Copyright © 1973, 1978, 1984, 2011 by Biblica, Inc.™ Used by permission of Zondervan. All rights reserved worldwide. www.zondervan.com The "NIV" and "New International Version" are trademarks registered in the United States Patent and Trademark Office by Biblica, Inc.™

Scripture quotations marked KJV are taken from the King James Version.

Scripture quotations marked ASV are taken from the American Standard Version.

Scripture quotations marked NKJV are taken from the New King James Version. Copyright © 1982 by Thomas Nelson. Used by permission. All rights reserved.

Scripture quotations marked NLV are taken from the New Life Version. Copyright © Christian Literature International. Used by permission. All rights reserved.

Scripture quotations marked HCSB are taken from the Holman Christian Standard Bible®, Copyright © 1999, 2000, 2002, 2003, 2009 by Holman Bible Publishers. Used by permission. Holman Christian Standard Bible®, Holman CSB®, and HCSB® are federally registered trademarks of Holman Bible Publishers.

Scripture quotations marked ESV are from the ESV® Bible (The Holy Bible, English Standard Version®), copyright © 2001 by Crossway, a publishing ministry of Good News Publishers. Used by permission. All rights reserved.

Scripture quotations marked NASB are taken from the New American Standard Bible® (NASB), Copyright © 1960, 1962, 1963, 1968, 1971, 1972, 1973, 1975, 1977, 1995, 2020 by The Lockman Foundation. Used by permission. www.Lockman.org

Edited by Annette LaPlaca
Interior design: Ragont Design
Cover design: Erik M. Peterson
Cover painting: *Nocturne—Blue and Gold* by James Abbott McNeill Whistler
Author photo: Jessica Delgado Photography

Library of Congress Cataloging-in-Publication Data

Names: Thompson, Jessica, 1975- author.
Title: How God loves us : 40 days to discovering his character in the fruit
   of the Spirit / Jessica Thompson.
Description: Chicago : Moody Publishers, [2022] | Includes bibliographical
   references. | Summary: "Can it be that the fruits of the Spirit listed
   in Galatians 5 are the characteristics of God-and He loves us with those
   attributes? In 40 readings designed for daily devotions, Jessica
   Thompson takes you across the whole Bible to reveal the loving character
   of the triune God"-- Provided by publisher.
Identifiers: LCCN 2021038695 (print) | LCCN 2021038696 (ebook) | ISBN
   9780802424372 (paperback) | ISBN 9780802499974 (ebook) | ISBN
   9780802400000
Subjects: LCSH: Fruit of the Spirit. | God (Christianity)--Love. |
   Bible--Criticism, interpretation, etc. | BISAC: RELIGION / Christian
   Living / Personal Growth | RELIGION / Christian Theology / Soteriology
Classification: LCC BV4501.3 .T4726 2022 (print) | LCC BV4501.3 (ebook) |
   DDC 234/.13--dc23
LC record available at https://lccn.loc.gov/2021038695
LC ebook record available at https://lccn.loc.gov/2021038696

Originally delivered by fleets of horse-drawn wagons, the affordable paperbacks from D. L. Moody's publishing house resourced the church and served everyday people. Now, after more than 125 years of publishing and ministry, Moody Publishers' mission remains the same—even if our delivery systems have changed a bit. For more information on other books (and resources) created from a biblical perspective, go to www.moodypublishers.com or write to:

Moody Publishers
820 N. LaSalle Boulevard
Chicago, IL 60610

1 3 5 7 9 10 8 6 4 2

Printed in the United States of America

To the women at RISEN Church

Contents

Kindness

Goodness

Faithfulness

Gentleness

Whose Fruit?

When you hear the phrase "Fruit of the Spirit" what comes to mind? Is it a pithy kid's song you learned when you were in Sunday school? Is it a series of words you would never use to describe yourself? Is it a to-do list? Is it a way for you to assess other people to judge if they are true believers? Does it make you roll your eyes because you feel how far you fall short? Are you going through the words now to consider if you are advancing in any of them? Maybe you have never heard the phrase *fruit of the Spirit* before in your life. Or maybe you are like me and somehow your brain takes you to a very weird place and you think "Fruit of the Loom" instead, suddenly picturing the group of fruit-costumed, smiling people, and you can't help but smile. Whatever the case may be, I am glad you picked up this book.

This forty-day devotional is based on Galatians 5:22–23, which reads, "But the fruit of the Spirit is love, joy, peace, patience, kindness, goodness, faithfulness, gentleness, and self-control. The law is not against such things." A multitude of books have been written about these two verses, most of them centering on why Christians *should* display each of these fruit of the Spirit or *how to* display them. If we are Christ followers, the Holy Spirit is with us and living in us; as a result there should be evidence of that in our daily living. At the same time, I am certain that Christ followers continually fail to live up to this list—and will continue to fail fulfilling this list (Rom. 3:23). Because while the Spirit is absolutely at work in us (Rom. 8:11), the flesh is warring against that work (Matt. 26:41). The astounding proclamation of the gospel is that even though we do continue to fail, we are counted as righteous before a holy God because of the work that Jesus Christ did for us (Rom. 4:25). He is the perfect one who completely embodied all these attributes every single second of every single day of His life (1 Peter 2:22). If you believe, you are completely forgiven (1 John 1:9) and now are hidden in Christ's record so when God looks at you, He sees the perfection of His Son (Rom. 3:23–24). You continue to have the righteousness of Christ—even though you were impatient five minutes ago when you yelled at the person in the car in front of you because he was going too slow and you had places to be!

I hope to take us all on a journey deeper into the "Fruit of the Spirit" but not in a way that you have been taught about them before, if you have been taught about them at all. Self-aware people reading this book know, at some level, that they need more "love, joy, peace, patience, kindness, goodness, faithfulness, gentleness, and self-control" in their

> **As we behold the beauty of the Lord we will be changed.**

lives. So you won't hear a lot from me about how you need to do better or to try harder. The power to change doesn't come from looking inward. There is benefit to recognizing that you fall short, but only if that inward look leads to an upward look. The power to change comes from the Giver of the fruit— hence the biblical phrase *fruit of the Spirit*, not the *fruit of trying harder*. There are plenty of self-help books out there to give you great practical advice on how to be a more patient, loving, kind, self-controlled person, but there is only one gospel, only one God who can change the hearts of His children.

My goal is to show you the beauty of the triune God. I want to wow you with the loveliness of His character. I want you to read how He is by His very nature loving, joyful, peaceful, patient, kind, good, faithful, and gentle. As you learn about Him, I am praying your heart overflows with gratitude for who He is. That gratitude is one of the means the Holy Spirit will use to change your life. As we behold the beauty of the Lord we will be changed. We will become more like Him because we will see Him as He is.

On most days I go for a walk in a field close to my house. The field is owned by a nearby horse-boarder to grow hay to feed horses. There are a few trees in the field, but it is mostly just an open space. Typically, in the summer I walk early in the morning before it gets too hot. There are days that I can't make it out early, so I go when the sun is doing its best to show everyone who is boss. On those days that field is hot and dusty, and I watch for those few trees that promise a respite from the burning ball of gas that seems to exist just to beat me down. Once I get to the shade, my pace slackens. Many times I stop to rest before I finish the trail. The shade offers me exactly what I need before I keep going on my journey. That little break makes a huge difference. Yet on winter days when I am walking that exact same field, I hate having to walk through the shade of those trees. When I am cold, I take advantage of the pockets of sun that peek through the clouds. When I get to the shade, I hurry through it because I don't want to feel the chill.

My prayer is that as you read this book it will be exactly what you need. It will either be the break from the heat and trial that you are going through, that shade that you long for, that respite from the fire, or it will be the break in the clouds on that dreary day that brings you warmth. If you heart is cold toward God, my prayer is that this book will be the flint to start a fire in your heart again. I want you to rest when you read this, and I want you to simultaneously feel invigorated. I want you to be so taken by who God is that you are transported, even if just for a few minutes in your day, to a place of worship. So let's go on this walk together. Let's lace up our tennis shoes and journey out to the field where we can see why our God is so glorious.

LOVE

Motherly Love

*The L*ORD* passed in front of him and proclaimed:*
*The L*ORD*—the L*ORD* is a compassionate and gracious God,*
slow to anger and abounding in faithful love and truth.

EXODUS 34:6

Have you ever seen a first-time parent completely smitten with a baby? You know that mom must be utterly exhausted, sleep-deprived, and hormonal, but the way she looks at her little one exudes dedication and love. I remember feeling so in love with my firstborn that I would tear up just holding him close, rubbing his chubby little hands. I remember not wanting to be apart from him, even when he was asleep. Those feelings were there with my other two, but by then I was so busy that I wasn't afforded the luxury of reveling in my emotions.

Think of that tender, motherly type of love and read our verse again. "The

> **We are accustomed to thinking about God in terms of Father, but how often do we think of His love for us as tender or motherly?**

L<small>ORD</small> is a compassionate and gracious God, slow to anger and abounding in faithful love and truth." The word for love in these verses is also sometimes translated "tender mercies or compassions," from the word *womb* to connote a motherly type of love. We are accustomed to thinking about God in terms of Father, but how often do we think of His love for us as tender or motherly? Isaiah 49:15 says this: "Can a woman forget her nursing child, or lack compassion for the child of her womb? Even if these forget, yet I will not forget you." One of the most compassionate and devoted types of love that we know here on earth is between a mother and her child. God is saying that His love is so compassionate, devoted, sacrificial, and committed that it makes a mother's love look like one that is forgetful.

Martin Luther describes this type of love as "goodness in action." A good mother's love acts. She takes care of the needs of her child. She forgoes sleep and many of her own needs so she can devote herself to her child's well-being. God's love is an action-filled love. He takes care of your needs. He gave His very Son, His beloved Son, because of the depth of His love for us. His love isn't empty sentimentality. His love moves Him toward us.

The Lord's love is steadfast. It doesn't vacillate. His love isn't hot one day and cool the next. His love stays the same. God's love is always pursuing. He chooses to define His love this way because we doubt that He could continue to love us after what we have done, what we have thought, what we have looked at, what we have said. His love is able to look our unloveliness straight in the face and never even consider wavering in His devotion to us. He cannot waver; that is not who He is.

Today remember God's love for you. Think about His love in the terms He uses to describe it. Consider His tenderness toward you. Let that tender affection move you to love Him in return and to love others.

Be blessed by these words written by a Scottish pastor in the nineteenth century:

How soothing, in the hour of sorrow, or bereavement, or death, to have the countenance and sympathy of a tender earthly friend! . . . these words tell thee of one nearer, dearer, and tenderer still—the Friend who never fails—a tender God! By how many endearing epithets does Jesus exhibit the tenderness of His affection to His people!

Does a shepherd watch tenderly over his flock? "The Lord is my Shepherd!"

Does a father exercise fondest solicitude towards his children? "I will be a Father unto you!"

Does a mother's love exceed all other earthly types of affectionate tenderness? "As one whom his mother comforteth, so will I comfort you!"

Is the apple of the eye the most susceptible part of the most delicate bodily organ? "He keeps them as the apple of His eye!"

When the "Shepherd and Bishop of Souls" finds the sinner like a lost sheep, stumbling on the dark mountains, how tenderly He deals with him! There is no look of wrath—no word of upbraiding—in silent love "He lays him on His shoulders rejoicing!"[1]

Loved from Eternity Past

I have loved you with an everlasting love;
therefore, I have continued to extend faithful love to you.

JEREMIAH 31:3

Charles Spurgeon writes about this passage, saying, "He loved you without beginning. Before years, and centuries, and millennium began to be counted, your name was on his heart. Eternal thoughts of love have been in God's bosom towards you. He has loved you without a pause; there never was a minute in which he did not love you. Your name once engraved upon his hands has never been erased, nor has he ever blotted it out of the Book of Life."[2]

Love is who He is at His core.

It is God's very character to extend love to you. Love is who He is at His core. He loved you from eternity past and will love you into the eternal future. His love extends through time and space and beyond anything we will ever understand. He promises to continue in this faithful love for you.

Let's read our verse for today with more context of the whole chapter from Jeremiah: "The people who survived the sword found favor in the wilderness. When Israel went to find rest, the Lord appeared to him from far away. **I have loved you with an everlasting love; therefore, I have continued to extend faithful love to you**. Again I will build you so that you will be rebuilt, Virgin Israel. You will take up your tambourines again and go out in joyful dancing" (Jer. 31:2–4, emphasis mine). These verses are spoken to a people who knew suffering. They are described as a people who "survived the sword." It may be as you are reading this today you feel like you are just trying to survive the sword, or perhaps you are so freshly out of a time of suffering that you're still not sure if you survived or not. Maybe you are currently experiencing pain that seems to be taking the very life from you. You feel no rest. You feel no joy. You only know tears and heartache.

Your heavenly Father's message to you today reminds you that you are loved. You are not loved in a standoffish manner. You are loved with a warm, everlasting love. These verses do not say, "To all the people who survived the sword, see, it wasn't all that bad. You made it. Stop complaining. You should have trusted Me more." No, that is not how God relates to us. He acknowledges the suffering. He doesn't minimize it. He calls it as it is. "You survived the sword." The Lord sees that you are in the wilderness. He doesn't say, "This isn't a bad spot at all! Just have a better outlook, and you will see this isn't actually a wilderness at all—it's an oasis!" No, the Father recognizes that the place you are in is difficult. He doesn't try to pretty it up or put a good spin on it.

Yet God declares that we find favor even there. We find the outlandish favor of His love—the favor of a Father whose love is not dependent on how we are dealing with our circumstances but depends only on who He is. He sees that we need to be rebuilt. He sees we need restoration, and He promises to bring that. He knows that real hardships strip us of our joy. He doesn't tell us that joy isn't important or that we should just suck it up; instead He gives us the hope of "joyful dancing." We may not fully experience the joyful dance in this lifetime, but for certain in eternity to come we will know joyful dance in a way we never even imagined. Then we will fully realize what His faithful love means for us. We will dance because we will see how His love has kept us. We will dance with all the other wilderness wanderers and rejoice because of the love of our God.

God Loved

For God loved the world in this way: He gave his one and
only Son, so that everyone who believes in him will not perish
but have eternal life.

JOHN 3:16

God loved. This is the beginning and the completion of our faith. These two words give us hope and fill us with joy. God, the Creator of the universe, the one who was and is and is to come, the giver of life, the sustainer of all things, majestic in holiness, beautiful, wonderful, splendid—this God *loved.* He feels affection for, His heart is drawn toward, His eyes are set up, His mind is full of thoughts of, He loves.

God loved *the world.* His heart is for the world. His love is for you. His love is for me. His love is for the sinner. His love is for the dust He took and reshaped into a man and into a woman. God loves those who reject Him. He loves those who disdain Him. He loves those who seek Him. He loves those who long for Him. He loves the world. This love comes from who He is. This love is bestowed upon the unlovely by the Lovely One. God is love.

God loved the world *in this way: He gave.* God's love is not static. God's love is not impotent. God's love moves Him to give. God's love moves Him toward us. God does not look at us with a cooled affection. God loves us and is moved into action. His love moved Him to give. His loved moved Him to sacrifice. His love moved Him toward us.

God loved the world in this way: He gave *His one and only Son.* God's love for us moved Him to give the most precious gift He could give. When we love we give, but we never give completely, we never give without some self-service, we never give without some self-protection, and we always hold a little bit back; our love

> **God gave His all: He gave Himself.**

is imperfect. When God loves He gives all. His love served us and cost Him. His love sacrificed His very self for us. He gave His Son. Spurgeon asks what more God could give: "When the great God gave his Son he gave God himself, for Jesus is not in His eternal nature less than God. When God gave God for us he gave himself. What more could he give? God gave his all: he gave himself. Who can measure this love?"[3]

God loved the world in this way: He gave His one and only Son, *so that everyone who believes in Him will not perish but have eternal life.* He loved and gave so we would not perish. He loved and gave so that we could live eternally. He loved and gave so we could be with Him forever. Our past, present, and future are changed because of His love for us. All we have to do is believe—believe God is as good as He says He is, believe He loves us the way He claims to, believe that all we must do is receive.

This verse is perhaps the best-known of all the verses from God's Word. Think on this well-loved verse today and about what great love God has for you. Consider how that love moved Him to give. Remember what that love moved Him to give. God's love for you has changed everything. Believe that love is for you today.

Loved Completely

I live by faith in the Son of God,
who loved me and gave himself for me.

GALATIANS 2:20

The apostle Paul's declaration in this verse makes my heart explode with happiness. Jesus, the Son of God, loves me and gave Himself for me.

Who loved me?

Jesus, the Son of God. To be loved by anyone, truly loved, is a cause for happiness. But to be loved by Jesus is a cause for exultation. Read and take hold of how Jesus is described in Colossians 1:18–20: "He was supreme in the beginning and—leading the resurrection parade—he is supreme in the end. From beginning to end he's there, towering far above everything, everyone. So spacious is he, so expansive, that everything of God finds its proper place in him without crowding. Not only that, but all the broken and dislocated pieces of the universe—people and things, animals and atoms—get properly fixed and fit together in vibrant harmonies, all because of his

God isn't detached when He thinks about you. His heart yearns to be in relationship with you.

death, his blood that poured down from the cross" (MSG). This One with infinite power and worth—this is the One who holds you in His heart.

What did He do?

He loved you. Take each of these words and think on them individually. He loved *you*. He doesn't just tolerate you. He doesn't just think of you fondly. He doesn't just hope for the best for you. He loved you. This word *love* is full of emotion. God isn't detached when He thinks about you. His heart yearns to be in relationship with you. He wants you to know about His love for you and to live a life propelled by that knowledge.

What did His love cause Him to do?

Jesus gave His life for you. His love isn't just sentimentality. More than deep feelings, God's love is action. His love moved Him to give not just His heart but His entire self. He did this so we could have perfect relationship with God and so we could love others with the love we have been shown.

The entire book of Galatians is devoted mainly to reminding us that our work isn't what saves us but rather that Jesus' work on our behalf is what makes us whole. Paul writes this letter to remind the people of Galatia to stop working to earn their salvation and to stop working to try to earn love. We need to hear that message every single day as well because so much of our lives is spent trying to prove to God and to others that we really are worth being loved. Jesus puts a stop to that. He says, "I love you because I do. I love you in the fullness of who I am. I love you and will give Myself to you because even on your best days you fail at giving yourself to Me." This type of love changes us.

John Flavel, an author and pastor from the seventeenth century, wrote,

"The Son of God, who *loved* me and *gave* Himself for me!"
    Galatians 2:20
Out of Christ's condemnation—flows my justification!
Out of His agony—comes my victory!
Out of His pain—comes my ease!
Out of His stripes—comes my healing!
Out of His gall and vinegar—comes my honey!
Out of His curse—comes my blessing!
Out of His crown of thorns—comes my crown of glory!
Out of His sin-atoning death—comes my eternal life!
O what a melting consideration is this![4]

When we focus on God's great love, the Holy Spirit moves our hearts to love others. We can't help but want to spread that love. Then even on the days when we resist His work, Jesus, the Son of God, continues to love us and to remind us that He gave His life for us.

Beloved Children

*See what great love the Father has given us
that we should be called God's children—and we are!*

1 JOHN 3:1

What glorious truths are proclaimed by this verse! John is so excited about what he is about to tell you that he makes sure to get your full concentration. He starts out by saying, "See!" Sometimes this is translated *look* or *behold*. It's as if John takes our face between his two hands, makes intense eye contact, and says, "This is really important. Make sure you are paying attention." Then he goes on to talk about the Father's love for us.

"See what great love the Father has given." Our Father is abundantly generous with His love. He has loved us from eternity past. He loves us completely now. He has promised to love us into eternity future. He has given this love because it is His character to love. First John 4:8 tells us that "God is love." Love existed in the Trinity before creation and because that love could not be contained within the Trinity, the triune God created us so that He could share that love with us. His love is effusive. His love is eternal. His love never gives up on us. His love never stops.

Maybe you have not spent a lot of time thinking about the concept of the Trinity. That term refers to our triune God, meaning we believe in one God in three beings—the Father (God), the Son (Jesus Christ), and the Holy Spirit. These three are equal in worth and power. They rejoice in each other and love each other completely. They are the truest definition of unity. They are all working for the good of the others because they understand they are One.

How does God's love change us? "See what great love the Father has given us that we should be called God's children—and we are!" His love re-creates us into dearly loved and welcomed children. A theologian who writes especially about the love of the triune God, Michael Reeves says,

> God welcomes and embraces us as children, never to send us away. (For children do not get disowned for being naughty.) He does not offer some kind of "He loves me, He loves me not" relationship whereby I have to try and keep myself in his favor by behaving impeccably. No, "to all who received Him, to those who believed in his name, he gave the right to become children of God" (John 1:12)—and so with security to enjoy His love forever.[5]

The Father's great love that He so freely gives is ours today. We can rest in the security of His love. We are safe in His love. Maybe you have never known a love that makes you feel safe, maybe you have never known a love that makes you feel as though you can rest. The Father's love is that love. You are never on thin ice with Him. You never have to make up for the off day you had yesterday to somehow get back into His good graces. His good grace is yours right now forever. You will not be disowned because the Father loves you as He loves the Son and He will not disown Himself. He is faithful.

> You never have to wonder what your Heavenly Father thinks or if His affection is offered only out of obligation.

You may have felt as though you had to earn your earthly father's love. You may still feel that way. Perhaps you never knew your father. Maybe you feel as though your father just tolerates you or wishes you were someone else or something other than you are. Maybe you have a great father, but you still sometimes wonder what he thinks of you. You never have to wonder what your heavenly Father thinks or if His affection for you is offered only out of obligation. He is thoroughly thrilled to have you as His family.

God is a good Father. He delights in His children. He delights in loving His children, and that is who we are! We are enveloped into the love the Trinity shares amongst itself. We have been caught up into this rapturous, divine love, and we will never be without it.

JOY

Joyful Strength

Do not grieve, because the joy of the LORD is your strength.

NEHEMIAH 8:10

I grew up in the church, and I heard this verse preached on and talked about on many different occasions. Whether it was what was being taught or what I heard, I always understood this verse to mean that if I could just be happy because of God then I will be strong and do all the things that I need to do to be a good Christian. As a result, these words always ended up being a source of more discouragement rather than a source of joy. I would think, "Okay! I am going to act happy all the time, and then I will be strong!" Inevitably, I would end up being sad about something or just not happy-go-lucky and then I would feel guilty that I wasn't having the "joy of the Lord." Feeling like a failure, I'd distance myself from God. Then I would not experience joy when I thought about God; instead I would experience grieving and sadness.

This verse is too often ripped out of context and preached as a stand-alone verse. The context, what was happening his-torically when this was said, gives this verse its beauty and power. So let me give you a little bit of history. If history is not your jam, I promise this will be quick and worth your time. If history is your jam, you should spend some time outside of this devotional studying what was happening in the book of Nehemiah.

The Israelites were in a time of exile. The beautiful temple that Solomon built and their holy city had been broken down and destroyed. Nehemiah had asked King Artaxerxes for permission to rebuild the walls of Jerusalem. He was granted his wish. Once the walls and gates were rebuilt, Ezra, a fellow prophet at the time, gathered all the Jews together. He read them the law of God. The people sat and listened to all the ways they had failed God. They had restored the broken walls of their city, but now they saw that they were broken people and they needed restoring as well. As this realization was settling in, they were grieving because they hadn't lived as they were supposed to live. They had failed to love God and failed to love others. And that's when the truth of this verse comes swooping in to rescue them.

The people are crying because of the brokenness they recognize in themselves and each other. And Nehemiah says,

God is calling us into His own celebration and joy.

"'This day is holy to GOD, your God. Don't weep and carry on.' They said this because all the people were weeping as they heard the words of The Revelation. He continued, 'Go home and prepare a feast, holiday food and drink; and share it with those who don't have anything: This day is holy to God. Don't feel bad. The joy of GOD is your strength!'" (Neh. 8:9–10 MSG).

Nehemiah wasn't talking about mustering up some fake happiness so people think you are a strong Christian. This verse is about reveling in the forgiveness and grace of God. This verse is about celebrating that it brings God joy to forgive us and welcome us even though we have broken the law. When we meditate on the fact that we are forgiven we can't help but feel joy. God's joy in redeeming us is contagious. When we feel the joy and relief that comes from forgiveness, we have the strength to continue on. We have strength to try again even though we fail over and over again. God is calling us into His own celebration and joy. Grieving over our sin is important and good, but we should never stay there because that isn't what God wants for us or from us. He wants us to rejoice and join in the eternal joy that is who He is and what He is all about.

Ours is a joyful God, and He wants to make us a joyful people. God isn't interested in a people who pretend everything is okay when it really isn't. He wants a people who look at their circumstances and reach deep into the heart of joy that their God has in redeeming them. He wants their joy to come from being a forgiven people, a forgiven people who want to invite others into the party: "Go home and prepare a feast, holiday food and drink; and share it with those who don't have anything." God's joy is contagious, and that makes our joy contagious and generous, ready to share. The really great news is that even on the days when you don't feel joyful or you don't want to share your feast, God is still rejoicing over you and forgiving you and loving you. Rejoice!

Rejoiced Over

No longer will they call you Deserted,
or name your land Desolate.
But you will be called Hephzibah,
and your land Beulah;
for the LORD will take delight in you,
and your land will be married.
As a young man marries a young woman,
so will your Builder marry you;
as a bridegroom rejoices over his bride,
so will your God rejoice over you.

ISAIAH 62:4–5 NIV

We called my grandmother on my father's side "Candy Grandma" because she gave us candy every single time we visited. She'd say hot dogs were her "favorite fruit." When I would take my kids to visit her, I would go at times of the day where one wouldn't typically eat a meal because I didn't want her to go to the trouble of preparing something for us, but inevitably we would end up eating a second lunch because she insisted on "having a party." This woman who informed and shaped me in a multitude of ways often called me *Hephzibah*. I had no idea what it meant at the time, and it was normal for her to make up words (*Hootsycadoodle* was one of her favorite expressions when she was happily surprised, for example) so I didn't think much of it. Then one day I was reading my Bible and I came across Isaiah 62:4–5. I saw the word *Hephzibah,* and I was astonished. There was a tiny *a* next to it, so I went racing down the page to find out what *Hephzibah* meant. At the bottom of the page was a definition that broke me and thrilled me all at once: "My delight is in her." Every time Candy Grandma called me by this nickname she was telling me she delighted in me. To be loved so deeply by a grandparent is a wonderful gift.

You may have experienced a love like that from a grandparent and understand what I am talking about, or maybe you haven't experienced a love like that and are grieved or even angry that you haven't known that feeling. To those who know that love and to those who don't, we have a God who says those words about us. His delight is in us. We may feel "deserted" or "desolate," but God changes us by His wonderful love and we are called "my delight is in her." We are not alone any longer. If that truth weren't magnificent enough, we are loved by God as a young man who marries a young woman. His love for us is consuming. His love for us gives Him delight. His love for us gives Him joy. He is a joyful God because of how He feels about you and me.

So many of us think that God is disappointed in us or that He just tolerates us. We know He loves us, but we entertain a sneaking suspicion that He loves us because He has to. These verses tell those thoughts to "Hush up" (another of Candy Grandma's favorite sayings).

Your God rejoices over you! My God rejoices over me. Our God rejoices over us! How is this true? I literally shake my head in wonder over this truth. Tears well in my eyes because I just can't believe it is true. But to my own doubt and to yours, I echo my grandma, "Hush up."

We must choose to believe what God says, and He says He delights in us.

We must choose to believe what God says, and He says He delights in us. What a tremendous sense of relief and happiness and joy that brings to my tired, anxious heart. I pray it does the same for you, filling you with the fullness of joy today. I pray that you extend that joy to everyone you encounter today. I pray that His joy in us spills over into the whole world so we might all know the unspeakable pleasure of knowing we are delighted in because our God is just that good.

Joy in My People

And I will rejoice in Jerusalem, and joy in my people: and the voice of weeping shall be no more heard in her, nor the voice of crying.

ISAIAH 65:19 KJV

Have you ever felt a physical pain in your heart because you were so happy? When I was pregnant with my firstborn, I remember rubbing my belly and feeling that my heart was going to explode with love and joy. Then when he was born, I remember looking at him in complete awe and wonder, taking joy in having him safely in my arms. My delivery was chaotic and scary. After long, unproductive hours of labor, the baby's heart rate was dropping rapidly while my blood pressure went to the other extreme, climbing high. Doctors and nurses rushed in and out and talked quietly to one another. Decisions were made. I signed a document I don't even remember reading. I drank some awful tasting liquid, and they wheeled me into an operating room where oldies from the band Cream were playing full blast. I ended up having an emergency C-section. It felt completely surreal and as if it all happened in a matter of five minutes. I saw my baby for a few brief seconds after delivery, and then I had to be separated from him while they finished with me. It felt like an eternity before they finally brought my son to me, and I got to hold him. My little son had done nothing to make me love him. He had not performed in any way. He had done nothing good or bad, and yet I was completely taken by him. I was overwhelmed with love for him, and he hadn't even looked at me yet.

This is how God takes joy in us. He rejoices in us just because we are alive and we are His. Let yourself stop and imagine God delighting in you like a parent delights in a newborn baby. He takes joy in your existence. As wonderful as that thought is, His joy is more profound than that. Our God knows everything about us. He knows all the things that should make Him turn from us or be displeased, and yet we read that He "will rejoice in Jerusalem, and joy in [His] people" (KJV).

His joy in us is deeper than a performance-based joy. We all know the kind of joyful pleasure that occurs when someone we love does something exceptional and we are happy for them. If the loved one's actions benefit you, your joy is increased. God's joy in us is disconnected from our performance. God's joy in us exists because of the work of Jesus Christ on our behalf. We have become His "beloved [child], with whom [He is] well-pleased" (Matt. 3:17). We have been hidden in the life Jesus lived, and God feels joy when He thinks of us.

Today's verse about God taking joy in His people appears in a passage about what the new heavens and the new earth will be like. Read Isaiah 65:17–20 for this short description of what we will experience for eternity, and it will build joy in your heart. God promises us that we will experience joy and then goes on to talk about how our joy ignites more joy in Him. Here is what John Calvin wrote about this passage: "He expresses more than in the preceding verse; for by these words he means that he not only will

God's joy in us is disconnected from our performance.

give to men ground for rejoicing, but even will be a partaker with them in that joy. So great is his love toward us, that he delights in our prosperity not less than if he enjoyed it along with us. And hence we obtain no small confirmation of our faith, when we learn that God is moved, and so powerfully moved, by such an affection toward us. If we are in painful and distressed circumstances, he says that he is affected by grief and sorrow; and, on the other hand, if our condition is pleasant and comfortable, he says that he takes great pleasure in our prosperity."[1]

God's joy is complete when our joy is flourishing. So today when you wonder if anyone cares what you are going through, when you wonder if there is anyone who feels joy when they think of you, remember these verses. Remember the joy the Lord experiences when He thinks of you; let that thought create joy in your own heart as you think of Him.

Joy in the One

*There will be more joy in heaven over one sinner who repents than
over ninety-nine righteous people who don't need repentance.*

LUKE 15:7

Today's Scripture, Luke 15:7, comes at the end of the parable
of the lost sheep. A parable is a short story Jesus told in order
to explain something that holds a deeper meaning. In Luke
15:1–7 Jesus tells the story of a shepherd who loses one of his
sheep and goes out to look for it. When he finds the sheep, he
rejoices and carries it home. Jesus told this story in response to
the Pharisees calling Him a "friend of sinners." The Pharisees
did not mean this as a compliment. They thought Jesus was
hanging out with all the wrong people. They were right. Jesus
seemed to love the company of scoundrels. The Pharisees were
wrong in assuming that Jesus was interested in only being
around people considered "good" by the religious community.

Often we are mistaken about who makes Jesus happy as
well. We tend to think those who follow all the rules and follow
even more rules than all those rules are the ones who make

Jesus and the inhabitants of heaven rejoice. But this story (and also the two parables that follow as you keep reading in Luke 15) tells us what really brings Jesus joy: when sinners, the ones who do everything wrong, repent and come home to the Father. The triune God's joy is complete and made to overflow when a sinner realizes she needs a Savior. When I sin, especially when it is a sin I continually give in to, I tend to feel ashamed and think, "Surely God is sick of me asking for forgiveness for this. He must be so disappointed in me. I am disappointed in myself." My default thinking is that God will forgive me, but He will do it because He has to. These verses tell a different story, reorienting our thoughts to remind us that God is not like us. When we repent God is joyful! Repentance is just agreeing with God about who He says He is and who He says we are. In His perfection, God knows the best way for us to live. We fail at that constantly and need a Savior. When we turn back to Him and agree with Him, He doesn't look at us with pity or with disdain or with an I-am-glad-you-finally-came-to-your-senses look. He looks at us with delight, joy, and love. The heavens are a place of joy because of sinners who repent and come home to the Father. We have no reason to hold back when it comes to admitting we have failed Him. God is not only ready to receive us, but He is joyfully running to welcome us (Luke 15:11–24).

> God is not only ready to receive us, but He is joyfully running to welcome us.

J. C. Ryle, a nineteenth-century Anglican bishop, said this about these verses from Luke 15:

There is an infinite willingness on God's part to receive sinners. However wicked a man may have been—in the day that he really turns from his wickedness and comes to God by Christ—God is well-pleased. God has no pleasure in the death of the wicked—but God has pleasure in true repentance.

Let the man who is *afraid* to repent consider well the verses we are now looking at, and be afraid no more. There is nothing on God's part to justify his fears. An *open door* is set before him. A *free pardon* awaits him. "If we confess our sins—then God is faithful and just to forgive our sins, and cleanse us from all unrighteousness" (1 John 1:9).

Let the man who is *ashamed* to repent, consider these verses, and cast shame aside. What though the world mocks and jests at his repentance? While man is mocking—angels are rejoicing! The very change which sinners call foolishness—is a change which fills Heaven with joy.

Have we repented ourselves? This, after all, is the principal question which concerns us. What shall it profit us to know Christ's love—if we do not use it? "If you *know* these things—blessed are you if you *do* them" (John 13:17).[2]

So run to your Father today. Confess what needs to be confessed. Then remember God at that very moment is taking joy in your repentance. He is taking joy because you trust His promise to forgive. He is taking joy in you.

Looking Forward

*For the joy set before him he endured the cross, scorning its
shame, and sat down at the right hand of the throne of God.*

HEBREWS 12:2 NIV

America has a dark and deep-rooted history of racism. At
the inception of our country, slavery was not just tolerated
but celebrated and deemed as necessary. Men, women, and
children made in the image of God and worthy of respect
and freedom were treated as nothing more than animals and
denied their God-given right to liberty all because of the
color of their skin. Something that has always confounded
me was that while slaves worked, they sang spirituals—songs
of hope, songs about Jesus, songs about the goodness of God
and the promise of heaven. Enslaved people sang these songs
to remind them of their truer reality, because it gave them
hope in the darkest of times. Dante Stuart says,

> The writers of these spirituals loved those good doctrines of
> God and his gospel. Out of their love of these truths came

the understanding that the Christian life was to be lived in the context of suffering with a hope that rises above and goes through affliction. Suffering was a fact of life and this fact came through the lyrics of the song. . . . Though slavery was a reality, it was not how the story ended.[3]

Slaves sang spirituals so they could be reminded of the joy they knew to be true and the joy of their eternity.

Jesus, in a sense, also sang a spiritual to remind Himself of the joy that awaited Him after the cross. What helped our Savior endure the pain of the cross? Knowing what was waiting for Him on the other side. It wasn't just the pain of the cross He endured. It was the pain of saying no to temptation every single day of His life. It was the pain of loving and being rejected. It was the pain of healing and being accused of being Satan. It was the pain of this broken world we are all so familiar with.

We were the joy set before Jesus.

Jesus endured that pain by looking forward to the joy of a redeemed people. He endured that pain knowing one day all would be made right and we would be His without anything hindering our love for Him. We were the joy set before Him. Our names were the words to the spiritual He sang to make it through the shame of the cross.

Jesus endured the pain. And don't be mistaken: He experienced every aspect of pain because He didn't distract Himself or anesthetize Himself. He entered into the pain because He knew the joy was coming. The heart of the Father to gather His family and welcome them home propelled that joy.

Jesus knew that what awaited Him was a seat next to His Father and a people who were loved and who loved in return. He knew what joy was coming, and it's a joy we will all enter into—a pure joy, an undefiled joy, a complete joy. The triune God experiences this joy every day because of who He is and what He has done. This joy is ours in part today, but one day it will be ours fully.

So today, sing your spiritual of joy in anticipation. Let your heart imagine what it will be like to be with Him. Let your eyes see your Savior who has long awaited your homecoming. One day, beloved, our joy will be complete.

PEACE

Shalom

For a child will be born for us, a son will be given to us . . .
He will be named . . . Prince of Peace.

ISAIAH 9:6

In the beginning God created. There was perfect relationship between God and what He created, perfect relationship between each human, perfect relationship between the creation (nature, animals, etc.) and the humans, perfect relationship within the humans' own inner workings. *Peace* is another word we can use for this perfect relationship. There was peace with God, peace with others, peace with creation, and peace within ourselves.

But you know the story well: Peace was destroyed by disobedience. Now everywhere we look we see the effects of that destroyed peace. We see it in our relationship with God. We see it in our relationship with others. We see it in our relationship with creation. We see it in our relationship with ourselves. There is brokenness wherever we look. We are set on using instead of loving. We are set on advancing ourselves instead of pushing others ahead. We are set on gaining instead of giving. We are set on fighting instead of making peace. And into this world of broken peace (*shalom*), God gives us a Son. A child is born for us, a child whose name is *Prince of Peace.*

We can often make this idea of *shalom* solely personal, thinking, "God sent Jesus to make peace with me." While that is a glorious truth and one worth meditating on, it isn't the whole glorious truth. A child was born for **us**, and a Son was given to **us**, to restore peace to every single area marred when Adam and Eve disobeyed. Jesus, our Prince of Peace, restores, reinvents, and revitalizes our relationship with God. We no longer mistakenly look at God as a cranky judge but now view Him clearly as a loving Father.

God also restores *shalom* in our relationship with others. We now no longer need to view others as stepping-stones to get ahead, or as pleasures to make us feel good about ourselves, or as pawns used to advance our agenda. Others are now image-bearers worthy to be treated with love because that is how our Prince of Peace has treated us.

This Prince of Peace changes how we relate to His creation as well. We don't look at the animals, the earth, and its resources only as objects to be destroyed and consumed without thought of damage done. Instead, the peace God has extended toward us changes the way we view the gifts we have been given. We are wise and faithful with them because God has been eternally kind in blessing us with such an amazing earth.

This peace also extends to how we deal with

> **We have permission to stop striving with ourselves and just rest in the goodness of His love and the security of our relationship with Him.**

ourselves. The inner turmoil we constantly feel is only quelled by our Prince who extends peace to us. His peace bleeds over into our lives, and we have permission to stop striving and fighting with ourselves and just rest in the goodness of His love and the security of our relationship with Him. His kingdom is a kingdom of peace. His ways are forever and always peaceful.

One of my favorite authors is Octavius Winslow, a nineteenth-century preacher in England and America. His words on this passage will bless you:

> The title belonging to our Lord Jesus we are now to consider is strikingly and impressively illustrative of His mission of love and reconciliation to our world. It was not on a mission of justly-deserved judgment that He came, but on *an embassy of undeserved mercy*. God would overcome man's evil with good. He might have blotted this apostate and rebellious world from the creation, assigning its place with the angels who kept not their estate, but are reserved in everlasting chains under darkness unto the judgment of the great day. But, O everlasting love, and discriminating grace! He set His heart upon man and resolved to become man—even the God-man Mediator; that He might save man. It is in the light of an embassy of *peace* that we are now to contemplate the Advent of the Son of God to our world. He came [as] an Ambassador of peace, plucked an olive-branch from the paradise of heaven, and sweeping across the dark waters of man's curse, bore that curse to the hill of Calvary, and dipping it in blood—His own

heart's blood—waved it before the eyes of a sinful and rebellious world, and proclaimed, "Glory to God in the highest, and on earth *peace* and good will to men!"[1]

Leaving

Peace I leave with you.

JOHN 14:27

If you have ever had a best friend tell you she was moving away, or heard your beloved pastor explain to the congregation that he has taken a job somewhere else, or had a family member explain why they can no longer stay in the city where you live, then you know the deep, gut-wrenching sorrow of loss of relationship. You may tell yourself and each other that nothing will change, that you will still stay in touch, that you will continue to make the relationship a priority. But you both know. You both know life will crowd out the space you wanted to create for the relationship. You both know things will inevitably be different.

The disciples were experiencing that gut-wrenching anticipation of loss as Jesus was explaining that He had to leave them (John 14). Although, truthfully, they had no idea the pain that awaited them. They didn't understand where Jesus was going or why they couldn't go with Him. Peter pressed Christ, asking if he could come with Him and promising he would follow Him anywhere even if it cost him his life. But Jesus told him again that separation was imminent. Can you imagine the confusion the disciples felt? They had centered their entire lives on being with Jesus because He had asked them to. They left jobs. They left families. They'd given everything to be close to Him; now He was telling them He was leaving.

The lovely part of Christ's character demonstrated in this narrative is that He didn't just say, "I am leaving. Suck it up. God is in control. It will be fine." He offered them something better; He offered them who He is. He tells them over and over again that He understands and sees their pain. He sees their truest need, and He promises to take care of them. He reminds them who He is and who God is. Then He says this: "Peace I leave with you. My peace I give to you. I do not give to you as the world gives. Don't let your heart be troubled or fearful" (John 14:27). Jesus leaves His peace with them.

What the disciples didn't understand is that the peace Jesus was promising them could only be fully theirs if He left them. He had to go do what He was born to do. He had finished part of His quest by spending thirty-three years doing everything to please His Father. Now He had this one last part to finish.

> **Our eternal peace only comes at Christ's expense, and He willingly gave His all.**

He had to die to obtain the peace He desired to give the disciples. He wanted to give them an eternal peace, not peace like the world gives, not a temporary distraction from the real problem. He desired to take care of their deepest problem once and for all.

Our eternal peace only comes at Christ's expense, and He willingly gave His all so we can experience this peace. Our sin earned war with God; Christ's death earned peace with God. Christ's death not only gives us peace with God, but it gives us peace with others and with ourselves. We no longer must fight to justify ourselves to others or to ourselves. The cross has said it all, and the resurrection proves that our great King has welcomed us into His family.

Today, as you are inevitably aware of all the different peace-robbers in your life, come back to our verse in John 14. Hear the words of your Savior to each of His disciples (including you). His peace is yours. His peace is different. His peace is better. His peace is eternal.

Peacemakers

Therefore, since we have been justified by faith,
we have peace with God through our Lord Jesus Christ.

ROMANS 5:1

Before we are saved by faith in Jesus, the Bible describes us as "once foolish, disobedient, deceived, enslaved by various passions and pleasures, living in malice and envy, hateful, detesting one another" (Titus 3:3). But now we are "a chosen race, a royal priesthood, a holy nation, a people for his possession, so that you may proclaim the praises of the one who called you out of darkness into his marvelous light" (1 Peter 2:9). How did this change come about? How did the one who was enslaved become the one who lives in marvelous light? Jesus is all holiness and goodness and beauty. We were all unholiness and darkness and ugliness. Yet Romans 5:1 tells us that everything has changed for us. We now have peace, the very peace that the Trinity experiences among Father, Son, and Spirit we now experience as well.

How did we become recipients of this peace? How do we have peace with God? The beginning of our verse for today explains it: "We have been justified by faith." There is so much gospel goodness packed into that little phrase. We have been justified. My mom, Elyse Fitzpatrick, describes justification like this: "Just as if I had never sinned. Just as if I had always obeyed." She might not be the first person to phrase it that way, but I have heard her say it so many times I have to give her the credit. Justification means we are right with God. When He looks at us, He sees us as completely forgiven. "Though your sins are scarlet, they will be as white as snow; though they are crimson red, they will be like wool" (Isa. 1:18). If that weren't enough to make you jump up and shout, "Hallelujah," God also tells us we are hidden in Christ. When He looks at us, He sees the perfect work of His beloved Son: "For you died, and your life is hidden with Christ in God" (Col. 3:3). We are forgiven and accepted.

> **We could never do enough good works to merit the peace of God, but—surprise of all surprises—He gives it to us anyway.**

We aren't forgiven and accepted because of anything we have done. We are justified by faith. We have gained a new status because we believe we needed one and that God has given it to us. We don't get this new status by some spectacular work or by being an Instagram Influencer or by being kind to the barista at Starbucks. We get this new status by faith, and that faith is a gift. We could never do enough good works to merit the peace of God, but—surprise of all surprises—He gives it to us anyway.

God in His essence is peace, wholeness, and *shalom*. Because He loves us, He wants to bring us into that perfect state of being. He does the work; we experience the *shalom*. Now because we have been gifted this peace, we go around and spread peace like butter on a warm piece of sourdough toast. We are peacemakers because of the Peacemaker. In your sphere of influence today, even if that space is small, spread the peace. Give it away. Remember how freely God has given His peace to you.

Guarded

And the peace of God, which transcends all understanding,
will guard your hearts and your minds in Christ Jesus. . . .
And the God of peace will be with you.

PHILIPPIANS 4:7, 9 NIV

Being completely transparent about who we are and what we think and feel often brings the exact opposite of peace. I wonder if anyone of us has ever been completely unmasked with our loved ones. We let certain people in on dark parts of our lives, hidden places, painful memories, but have we ever been wholly stripped bare? No filter? Just us?

Just before the writer Paul wrote today's passage about what will bring the peace of God into our lives, he wrote this: "Do not be anxious about anything, but in every situation, by prayer and petition, with thanksgiving, present your requests to God" (Phil. 4:6 NIV). Truly, we are aware

We experience the peace of God when we let go of all self-protection before Him.

that God knows our requests before we even know them, and yet here is this command to pray to make our requests known to God. Let Him in on everything. Why would God ask us to do this when He already knows? Because He wants us to trust Him enough to be completely open with Him. Walter Hansen writes,

> The condition for experiencing God's peace is not that God grants all of our requests but that we have made known all our requests to God with thanksgiving. God's peace is not the result of the power of our prayers or the effectiveness of our prayers. Prayer is not auto-suggestion, a form of self-hypnosis that produces God's peace. Prayer is our openness about our needs before God, our emptiness in his presence, our absolute dependence upon him with an attitude of constant thanksgiving and complete trust. When we pray with that attitude, the focus is not at all upon what we are doing or will do, but on what God will do. God will do something supernatural beyond our best abilities and thoughts: the peace of God will guard us."[2]

We experience the peace of God—we experience the character of God—when we let go of all self-protection before Him. We experience that peace because we trust that He accepts us as we are and loves us beyond measure. We have this peace because we believe God's promises to us and His disposition toward us. When we throw aside our imposter selves and become our true selves, God promises to guard us with His peace. Who He is guards who we are. The peace that He experiences in and of Himself becomes ours as we enter into deep relationship with Him.

Often we think of peace as only an inward frame of mind, but it most definitely does mean so much more. *Shalom* (peace) is also an outward frame. It is a love for neighbor because we have been loved. It is an extending of peace because peace has been extended to us. God's peace isn't stagnant; it flows, it moves, it redeems. Today you can experience this peace and give this peace away. Don't hide. Instead come clean before God in confidence, knowing you are a welcomed child. Relish this peace that surpasses everything we understand.

Tangible Presence

Now may the Lord of peace himself give you his peace at all times and in every situation. The Lord be with you all.

2 THESSALONIANS 3:16 NLT

The last couple of years have been a turmoil of constantly changing circumstances—with worldwide pandemic and mitigation parameters that changed week by week, with chaotic political upheaval. Our days have been rife with *maybes* and *what ifs*, and unfolding circumstances have often been dark and disappointing enough to make me shake my head and wonder what God is doing!

The word *peace* means "state of harmony or well-being"— basically the exact opposite of our national and world experiences just lately. And yet here is this wonderful verse in Thessalonians that calls us back to God. This type of verse is called a benediction. A benediction comes at the end of a letter, and it is typically a promise of a blessing. So read this verse as a promise. He will "pour into you his peace in every circumstance and in every possible way." I read that and I often think, *I feel lots of different emotions right now, but I can tell you that peace isn't one of them.* So how do I reconcile God's promise with emotional turmoil day by day?

I learn to define God by who He says He is and not by the circumstances I am experiencing. I tend to be so self-focused that whatever I am going through somehow ends up determining what I think of God. If I am experiencing a time of happiness and blessing, I tend to think of God as good and kind. If I am experiencing a time of sorrow and hardship I wonder if God cares. Maybe you can relate to this.

God asks us to take our eyes off what we see and to focus our minds and hearts on what we know is truth.

God calls us outside of ourselves. He asks us to take our eyes off what we see and to focus our minds and hearts on what we know is truth. The "Lord of Peace" is how God chooses to be identified here. The Greek word for the Holy Spirit can also mean "Comforter." Our comforter, our Lord of Peace who comes besides us in every situation and gently, consolingly reminds us that He is present, is near. I love that the verse says "may the Lord himself" give us peace. He does not send someone else to do the job. He is the one who wants us to join into the uninterrupted harmony that the Trinity experiences. The Lord is always inviting us to the goodness of who He is. He is the One drawing us closer to Him so we can know this peace.

Paul ends this letter to the church at Thessalonica with this promise: "The Lord's tangible presence be with you all."

May God's peace be tangible to you today. As who God is comforts us may we also comfort others. You do not have a God at war with you. You have a God who wants you to know and understand His peace and harmony. So we turn to Him today. We remember who He is. We remember He is close to us today and every day.

PATIENCE

Long-nosed

The LORD is slow to anger and abounding in faithful love,
forgiving iniquity and rebellion.

NUMBERS 14:18

The word that is translated "slow to anger" in this verse is literally *long-nosed*. Can you imagine if our verse read, "The Lord is long-nosed and abounding in faithful love"? The thought makes me smile. In the original Hebrew God made His heart known to His people using the word "nose." If God was angry, the Bible would talk about Him being "short-nosed." Basically, *short-nosed* is what we would call "short-tempered." *Long-nosed* meant that it took a lot to get God angry. I know people who live in a "long-nosed" way, but the difference is that once they get mad, goodness, do they ever get mad! But that is not how our God is. He is slow to anger *and* abounding in faithful love, forgiving iniquity and rebellion. He doesn't just ignore our sins or failures; He loves us enough to love us through them and forgive us.

This statement about God's abounding, faithful love comes to God's people right at yet another time when the

Israelites were being rebellious. God had brought them out of the slavery that they endured in Egypt and led them to the Promised Land. Once they got to the Promised Land, some spies went into the area to see if they could all live there. The majority of those spies came back with bad news. They reported that there were too many obstacles and even included a complaint about giants. But God had already promised His people that He would give them this land. Of course, like we do, the Israelites chose to believe the bad report from the spies instead of the promises of God. They didn't trust God. They didn't take Him at His word. So they decided they wouldn't go in. God was not happy with this decision and threatened to destroy them. However, Moses took the opportunity to remind God about His character. Moses is saying to God, "Remember who you are. You are slow to anger . . . long-nosed."

God is patient with you. He is patient with you in your disbelief and your mistrust.

Chad Bird, in his book *Unveiling Mercy,* says this: "The Greek word used to translate this Hebrew expression is found in 1 Corinthians 13:4, 'Love is patient.' Love is long-nosed. A Hebrew spin on 2 Peter 3:9 would be that the Lord is 'long-nosed toward you, not wishing that any should perish, but that all should reach repentance.' The long arm of God's law might accuse us, but the long nose of God's grace saves us."[1]

God is patient with you. He is patient with you in your disbelief and your mistrust. He is long-nosed toward you. He isn't a temperamental boss waiting for you to screw up so

He can yell at you. He is long-suffering. As you rejoice in that truth today, let it inform the way you interact with those around you. Ask the Holy Spirit to show you what it would be like if you were long in the nose. Remember that for all the times you have been impatient and unloving, our God loves you and deals patiently with you through your failure. Rest in His patience today.

Unfailing Patience

The Lord is compassionate and merciful,
slow to get angry and filled with unfailing love.

PSALM 103:8 NLT

I don't know if there is a task that requires more patience than teaching a child how to read. Or maybe I should say there isn't a task that tested my patience as much as teaching my children how to read. I homeschooled my kids for five years and then the Lord delivered me—thanks be to God. Don't get me wrong, on lots and lots of days I really loved homeschooling, but also on lots and lots of days I didn't. Homeschooling made me cry almost every day, either because there were moments of such intense beauty or there were moments of such intense horror. Teaching my children to read mainly fell in the horror category. It was difficult, in part, because once I had done all I thought I should do, I felt they should do their part. I had sat with them for hours and hours helping them to recognize each letter. I had taught them the sounds of those letters. We read so many beginning readers I had them all memorized. When I decided it was about time for my children to be reading flawlessly, every single molecule of patience left my body. I thought that the children didn't deserve patience anymore; what they deserved now was a stern voice and my unbending will for them to read without mistakes. The more pressure I put on them, the harder it was for them to read. The harder it was for them to read, the more I was disappointed in myself as a teacher and in them as students. Naturally, I responded by applying even more pressure. Well, I am sure you can imagine how it all ended—and it wasn't with thankfulness or perfect reading.

> **Our failures allow Him to show off His unmatched love for us.**

I am sure there are people in your life you think don't deserve your patience because "They really should get this by now!" The good news is that God never operates that way with us. Our Scripture passage describes Him as "patient with people who fail." I qualify as someone who God will be patient with because I continually fail. My guess is if you look at your life honestly you will see you qualify as well. We often think our failures disqualify us from receiving God's patience. We think that somehow God is only patient with people who deserve it, but the truth is none of us deserve it. Our failure is exactly what stokes His patience. Our failures allow Him to show off His unmatched love for us. He is bent toward showing us undeserved forbearance. If God was only going to show patience to those who deserved it or to those who didn't fail, then His patience would never be on display.

As you go about your day today and you determine who in your world deserves your patience and who doesn't, remember

God's patience with you. Remember how every one of your failures is a new way for Him to show His patience with you. Remember that His love for you is overflowing and that His patience with you doesn't have a limit. If God's patience had limits, you and I would already have exceeded those limits. He delights in showing His patience with you.

Yet Again

He will again have compassion on us;
he will vanquish our iniquities.
You will cast all our sins
into the depths of the sea.

MICAH 7:19

Chapter 7 of the book of Micah describes a bleak, realistic view of the world at the time. Micah let us in on how bad things really were. Here is a paraphrase of what he said:

> I'm overwhelmed with sorrow!
> > sunk in a swamp of despair!
> I'm like someone who goes to the garden
> > to pick cabbages and carrots and corn
> And returns empty-handed,
> > finds nothing for soup or sandwich or salad.
> There's not a decent person in sight.
> > Right-living humans are extinct.
> They're all out for one another's blood,
> > animals preying on each other.

They've all become experts in evil.
    Corrupt leaders demand bribes.
The powerful rich
    make sure they get what they want.
The best and brightest are thistles.
    The top of the line is crabgrass.
But no longer: It's exam time.
    Look at them slinking away in disgrace!
Don't trust your neighbor,
    don't confide in your friend.
Watch your words,
    even with your spouse.
Neighborhoods and families are falling to pieces.
    The closer they are—sons, daughters, in-laws—
The worse they can be.
    Your own family is the enemy. (Mic. 7:1–6 MSG)

Everything was wrong. There was no food. Every*one* was wrong. There was no one to trust. It sounds so horrific it is almost comical. But it was the reality Micah knew. Yet after all that sad description, our passage for today appears, making it all the sweeter. It proves God's patience all the more. In the darkest of times, in the worst circumstances, in the places where sin seems to reign without restraint, God is described as One who "will again have compassion on us; he will vanquish our iniquities."

God tells us over and over again that His patience is not something to be earned. It is not something we can coerce Him into showing to us. He is patient because that is who He is. And let's be honest: Patient is all He can be when dealing with a crew like us or a society like the one Micah described. God's only other option would be to wipe us out completely, and we know that He won't do that because He has promised not to (Gen. 9:11).

Why does God choose to "again have compassion on us"? Micah 7:18 provides

It makes God happy to show us how much He loves us.

the answer: "Who is a God like you, forgiving iniquity and passing over rebellion for the remnant of his inheritance? He does not hold on to his anger forever *because He delights in faithful love*" (italics mine). Passing over our sins, forgiving us repeatedly, casting our sins into the depths of the sea, keeping us for Himself—these bring Him delight. It makes God happy to show us how much He loves us.

God isn't just generally patient with humanity, although He is that. He is specifically patient with you. He knows your personal sins, He knows where you give in to temptation, He sees your heart, and He shows specific patience just when you are sure you don't deserve it.

We should delight in God's patience as He delights in it. We can look back on all the ways He has been patient with us and look forward to all the ways He will continue to be patient with us until the very end. He delights in outdoing what we can even fathom. We don't even understand the type of patience that God has with us because we don't even understand the depth of our sin. Yet again and again He will have compassion on us. Who is this God? He is ours. He is the One who delights to show His love to you. He is the One who delights to show

His patience with you. He is the One who you are free to run to today knowing you will receive mercy upon mercy and grace upon grace.

Homecoming Story

But I received mercy for this reason, so that in me,
the worst of them, Christ Jesus might demonstrate
his extraordinary patience as an example to those
who would believe in him for eternal life.

1 TIMOTHY 1:16

According to the Oxford dictionary, patience is defined as "the capacity to accept or tolerate delay, trouble, or suffering without getting angry or upset."[2] Even that definition makes me feel anxious, wondering if I have ever been truly patient a single day in my life. There are times when accepting or tolerating uncomfortable situations without getting angry or upset seems impossible.

Today's verse from 1 Timothy conveys Paul's account of his own salvation story. In the previous verses, Paul wrote about what type of life he had been living before the mercy of God came crashing in and saved him. You may or may not know about this man who wrote most of the books of the New Testament, but before he became a Christ follower, Paul was a

Christ-hater. He didn't just hate Christ in an abstract way that tends to be mostly apathetic. He hated Christ in an active way. He would murder anyone who agreed that Jesus was the Son of God. He would work to get Christians thrown into jail. He would torture those who loved Jesus. Then Acts 9 describes how Jesus paid him a visit with a conversation that turned his life around. Paul went from being the one who would persecute others because of their faith in Christ to the one being persecuted for his faith in Christ. Paul's own admission was that "'Christ Jesus came into the world to save sinners'—and I am the worst of them" (1 Tim. 1:15).

So why in the world would God choose to save Paul? Why would He take the "worst of sinners," a blasphemer and a hater, and make him His own? Paul answers that very question: so that "Christ Jesus might demonstrate His extraordinary patience." Truly Jesus perfectly fulfilled that definition of patience in His relationship with Paul. He accepted and tolerated all of the evil Paul acted out toward Him and His people. He tolerated it without repaying what Paul deserved. Instead of retaliating against Paul, God turned to him in mercy and kindness and loved him right into His family. Jesus looked at Paul with all of his anger and hatred and decided to love Paul.

Jesus forgives and welcomes in a celebratory way.

Jesus chose a person like Paul so we could be assured that no one is out of the reach of His love, kindness, and mercy. His patience stretches to the outermost hater of God. There is no one Jesus looks at and says, "Nope, not enough patience for that person's shenanigans." He takes the worst of us—He even took me, and He takes you—and He showers us with mercy and grace just because He loves to display how patient He is. His extraordinary patience wasn't just for Paul. His extraordinary patience is for you and me. He wants us to know that no matter what our past, no matter what our present, He is willing to forgive and welcome. He doesn't forgive and welcome in a begrudging way. He forgives and welcomes in a celebratory way. He celebrates His own good character. He celebrates you. He celebrates your homecoming.

Today might be a good day to recount your own salvation story. Remember all the times God displayed His patience toward you. Remember how and who you were apart from Him and celebrate who and how you are because of His renewing work in your life.

Delayed Promises

The Lord does not delay his promise, as some understand delay,
but is patient with you, not wanting any to perish
but all to come to repentance.

2 PETER 3:9

Have you ever been promised something, but the promiser didn't tell you when the promise would be fulfilled? You waited every day hoping today would be the day the promise was fulfilled.

When my kids were younger, we promised them a trip to Disneyland before the year ended—which, as a side note, wasn't a smart thing to do. Every single day they asked if today was the day. The kids were relentless. I am sure they were afraid we wouldn't follow through on our promise. As the year went on, the promise seemed more and more to them like empty words. When we finally made good on our promise, the kids were ecstatic! All the waiting they had done was quickly forgotten, and yet at the same time all the waiting had made the actual going even more exciting. The waiting built the anticipation, even though the waiting was very difficult.

Today's Scripture from 2 Peter overtly mentions God's patience with us, but in context this passage speaks to the patience we must exhibit. Jesus has promised to come again. He has promised that when He does come back, He will make everything right and restore all of creation to the fullness of what it was meant to be. He will bring *shalom,* or complete peace, to everything we know (1 Thess. 4:16–17; Matt. 16:27). We are anxiously awaiting that day. We cry out over and over again, "Come, Lord Jesus. Come." We don't understand the waiting. We don't understand why injustice after injustice continues to happen. We feel disappointed when evil continues to grow, seemingly unchecked. We don't understand these times we live in. We long for the time when our King will appear.

But our King is patient; He isn't quick to come back. Why? Because He is "not wanting any to perish but all to come to repentance." He is giving all of humanity time to repent. He is giving us the chance to admit we are sinners in desperate need of a Savior. Every day more sins are committed, every day more evils pile up—and yet He waits. He waits for the right time. He waits so that more and more people will come home to Him. The point of His patience is to give the hard-hearted time to respond.

God's patience draws us into His love.

We don't understand His timing, but God's Word tells us, "Dear friends, don't overlook this one fact: With the Lord one day is like a thousand years, and a thousand years like one day." Every day that we wait for His return our anticipation grows. Every day He doesn't come back should create in us a deep gratitude for all the lives saved that day. His patience draws us into His love.

So today as you live another day and see more evil and feel more heartache, remember that our God is patient. He wants more people to know His wonderful love. He shows His patience for our good and for the good of our loved ones. Rejoice in His patience today.

KINDNESS

Precious Lovingkindness

How precious is thy lovingkindness, O God!
And the children of men take refuge
under the shadow of thy wings.

PSALM 36:7 ASV

My dear grandmother died recently. She was ninety-seven years old and had lived an adventurous, extraordinary life. She had started getting out of bed less, except in the night when she would get up and fall. Her last fall started her down the end of her path here and toward her eternal home. On a Saturday we gathered with her, and we sang "Amazing Grace" and the Doxology. We recited the Lord's Prayer and took communion together. She was weak but alert. My grandmother sang with us and mouthed the words of the Lord's Prayer she had spoken so many times before. Then on Monday we were with her again, keeping vigil because we knew her end was near. She was sleeping and then suddenly moaned and opened her eyes. We all started proclaiming our love for her and telling her that she was free to go to Jesus, the One who loved her best. Then she left us. We all stood in awe of the great gift the Lord had given us—not just the gift of getting to experience those last few beautiful memories with her but the gift of having experienced her. Her proper, never too loud or too long laugh. Her beautiful piano playing. Her sweet words of "You are a wonderful caretaker," which she said to me every single Monday when I spent time with her. Her love for the color lavender. Her green thumb. Her notes, written in shorthand, that she left behind. Her love for ice-skating and classical music. My grandmother was truly a classy lady, which really stands in direct contrast to how anyone would ever describe me, which makes me appreciate her all the more.

In lovingkindness, the kind Father draws us close when we are broken-hearted.

While I'm thinking of my grandmother's life, which was yet another evidence of God's many loving gifts to me, the words of today's verse overwhelm me: "How precious is Thy lovingkindness, O God! And the children of men take refuge under the shadow of thy wings." I am overwhelmed by God's lovingkindness. I see it whenever I take the time to stop and look, or whenever the Holy Spirit breaks into my blindness to show me. God only ever shows lovingkindess to His children. The essence of who He is encapsulates kindness. He goes above and beyond to show us that He is near and He loves us. God accomplishes this so often by the people He places in our lives who point us to

Him. He shows His lovingkindness by filling our senses with the beauty of this world that He created for our enjoyment. He does it by giving us a place of refuge by His side and under His wing. In lovingkindness, He draws us close when we are broken-hearted. He is a kind Father. His kindness woos us and draws us near to His ever-loving heart. His kindness gives us security with Him.

Today as we contemplate how precious God's loving-kindess is to us, remember the ultimate act of kindness He has shown. He is our ongoing protection; He is our forever refuge. We can hide all of ourselves in Him, and He promises to cover us. Our dear heavenly Father sent His precious Son to cover every single one of our sins with His shed blood and to wash us completely clean so we can live lives marked by kindness. We can turn and show those next to us that kindness is something we value because our Father values it as well. By the work and the help of the Holy Spirit we can mirror and mimic God by being a place of shelter and refuge in this harsh, lonely world.

Life Giving

Because Your lovingkindness is better than life,
my lips shall praise You.

PSALM 63:3 NKJV

"That gives me life" is a saying that is making the rounds right now in my friend group. Someone sees a beautiful sunset and says, "That gives me life." A person tastes the delicious, warm sourdough bread drenched in butter and says, "That gives me life." A kid comes up out of nowhere and gives his mom a hug and tells her he loves her, and she says, "That gives me life." Finding a new restaurant, getting a new car, a win for a favorite team—the list of things that "give life" goes on and on. I'll admit I have used the phrase to convey my enjoyment, but I do know that short bursts of happiness are not actually giving life.

God's kindness is better than life.

The psalmist uses a variation of that phrase in our verse for today. "Your lovingkindess is better than life." God's kindness to us gives us life—actual life, everlasting life. His kindness is better than life. If everything else were taken away but we still had the kindness of our God, that would be enough. To know our Father is kind and cares for us is life itself.

God demonstrates His kindness in the way He watches over us. He knows the number of hairs on our heads. He is sympathetic toward us in our weakness. He promises to wash our scarlet sins white as snow. He promises never to leave us or forsake us. His love for us is unfailing, never-ending.

Let God's kindness toward you evoke a stream of praise from your heart. Dwell on His kindness to you in His creation, in sending His Son, in imparting the Holy Spirit. His kind heart is always and ever for you.

James Smith, a nineteenth-century pastor, wrote this about our verse:

> But what then, is *God's loving-kindness?* It is *His love displaying itself* in . . . kind words, kind acts, kind discoveries of His divine excellencies; feasting the soul with spiritual delights.
>
> *God's loving-kindness* is better than *life*, for . . .
> it bestows greater blessings,
> it confers higher honors,
> it imparts sweeter pleasures,
> it raises higher expectations,
> and it throws around us greater security.
> It is better, for . . .
> it is more lasting;
> it is more suited to the nature of the soul;
> it is truly glorious.

It is . . .
unmixed good,
unfading pleasure,
inexhaustible wealth![1]

Everlasting Kindness

"In a surge of anger,
I hid my face from you for a moment,
but with everlasting kindness
I will have compassion on you,"
says the LORD your Redeemer.

ISAIAH 54:8 NIV

In order for us even to begin to understand the fullness of
God's kindness toward us we need take a moment to be in
awe of His majesty and power. In order to be wowed by this
promise of "everlasting kindness," we need to be sobered by
His glory. So who is this God who claims kindness as part of
His character? This is the God whose words brought creation
into existence, the God who calls the stars by name, the God
who keeps the universe in perfect balance, the God who had
the creativity to think of the beauty and lightness of a hum-
mingbird and yet also created the massive and powerful gray
whale. This is the God who numbers and knows every grain of
sand. This is the God who has the power to stop the sun. This

is the God who controls every ruler of every kingdom in the entire world. This is the God who does whatever He pleases and claims that nothing is too difficult for Him. This is the God who stops the seas and pulls them back for His people. This is the God who promises that His kindness toward you compels His heart to move toward you in compassion.

God's kindness is not some weak, trivial thing with no power behind it. There have been times in my life where my children have seen me sad or hurting and have tried to make me feel better by being kind to me. When my "Candy Grandma" died, I was heartbroken in a way I had never known before. My children caught me crying on multiple occasions. On one of these occasions my youngest brought me a flower. This flower had already seen better days. Add to that the struggle it took for my kid to get it off the plant and into the house. By the time I had been given this gift of kindness, it was barely a stem with one petal on it. This kindness was sweet, though. The kindness made me smile, but it did nothing to stop my pain. My child's kindness did not hold very much power. But the kindness of our God isn't sweet sentimentality. His kindness changes everything for us. His kindness moved Him to become the Lord our Redeemer.

The scandalous surprise of God's kindness is that it extends to those who do not deserve it.

God's anger is but for a moment, and His kindness is everlasting. His character drives Him to draw you close. His kindness compelled Him to bring heaven down to earth in order to bring you back to heaven.

His kindness is not just reserved for those who are always doing the right thing. His kindness extends to those who have incited His anger. The scandalous surprise of God's kindness is that it extends to those who do not deserve it. This is not what we would expect from a holy God, but this is precisely who God says He is. Dane Ortlund writes, "The Christian life, from one angle, is the long journey of letting our natural assumption about who God is, over many decades, fall away, being slowly replaced with God's own insistence on who he is. This is hard work."[2] We continually have to confront our own ideas about God and our own tendency to insist that we live in a world of karma, where we get what we deserve. We must do the hard work to believe that God is motivated by kindness, that He is tender with us and toward us. Which is why this kindness should take our breath away when we take the time to consider it. As you consider His great kindness today, look for ways to share that same kindness with those in your life.

Kindness Is the Key

He also raised us up with him and seated us with him
in the heavens in Christ Jesus, so that in the coming ages
he might display the immeasurable riches of his grace
through his kindness to us in Christ Jesus.

EPHESIANS 2:6–7

I love the movie *The Princess Bride*. If you haven't seen it, you have my permission to take a couple of hours to watch it today. If anyone asks what you are doing, you can tell them it's homework for your study on the fruit of God's Spirit! In one scene in the movie, our hero, Westley, appears in an utterly hopeless situation—so hopeless he's actually dead, or so we think. Inigo Montoya, a sidekick of sorts, brings Westley to Miracle Max to see if he can bring him back to life. They lay Westley on the table, and Miracle Max asks why they want to bring him back to life. Inigo wants to avenge his father. Max cynically suggests that maybe Westley owes Inigo money. Miracle Max says he'll just ask Westley, to which Inigo replies, "He's dead, he can't talk." But Max comes back with,

"Ooohhh, look who knows so much. It just so happens that your friend here is only mostly dead. There is a big difference between mostly dead and all dead. Mostly dead is slightly alive. All dead—well, with all dead you can only do one thing: go through his pockets and see if there is any loose change." Max forces air into Westley's lungs and asks, "What do you have here that is worth living for?" Westley groans a breathy response: "True love!"

Unlike Westley, we weren't mostly dead. We were all dead, according to the beginning of Ephesians 2: "We were dead in our trespasses and sins." And yet like Westley, who is brought back to life because of true love, we are also made alive by the ultimate true love. It's not our own true love that saves us, but God's true love for us. His kindness is the conduit that makes us alive.

Grace changes everything; by grace you have been saved. You were made alive by God's love. You were raised up by His love. Why did He do this? Today's verse explains it: "so that in the coming ages he might display the immeasurable riches of his grace in kindness toward us in Christ Jesus."

God's grace doesn't run out. His kindness cannot be measured. It's too extreme to measure! That's what "immeasurable riches" means. He has extreme kindness toward you. If I asked most people what was extreme about God, the answer probably wouldn't be His kindness. Some would answer that God's restrictions on us are extreme or His judgments are extreme. Once again, these prevailing assumptions reveal that we don't have the right picture of who God is. It's human nature to think God's kindness is going to run out. I often feel as if this time God will have had enough of me and my failures, and He'll just be over it. But you know what is extreme about God? His kindness.

How is it possible for God to show us this mercy, kindness, and love? Grace operates in these verses over and over again: we are now "in Christ," we are together with Him, we have the best seats "in Christ," we have been shown this extreme kindness "in Christ," we have been created "in Christ." Because Christ lived the life we were commanded to live, and He died the death that we deserve, God purchased us.

He made the great exchange. He gave us His holiness and took our sinfulness. Christ's life, death, and resurrection **God's kindness is the key to our salvation.** changed our relationship with God. The grace and love that led Jesus from heaven to earth to Golgotha's hill is the grace that purchased reconciliation and keeps us in relationship with God.

It's all God's doing. It was His work to save us, His work to recreate us, and His work to keep us. His kindness is the key to our salvation.

At the Right Time

But when the kindness of God our Savior and his love for mankind appeared, he saved us—not by works of righteousness that we had done, but according to his mercy.

TITUS 3:4–5

The movie *Avengers: End Game* has a scene near the end that gets me hyped every time I see it. If you haven't seen it, here's your spoiler alert: I am about to reveal what happens. Near the end of the movie, it seems as if all hope is lost. Our heroes have battled valiantly, but Thanos has proved too strong for them. Thor, Captain America, and Iron Man are no match for Thanos. We look on helplessly as Captain America seems to accept his fate; he knows that he won't win, but he will fight. Then in the background, a portal opens and in walk Black Panther, Shuri, and Okoye, with an enormous army of Wakandan warriors behind them. Right then, in that moment, you know the tide has turned and that our heroes will save the day! Reinforcements showed up at just the right time.

Titus chapter 3 opens with the total mess we humans were in, describing us as "foolish, disobedient, deceived, enslaved by various passions and pleasures, living in malice and envy, hateful, detesting one another." But then the verse we're considering today comes along with that Black-Panther-in-the-End-Game excitement, and God's kindness appears: "When the kindness of God our Savior and his love for mankind appeared, he saved us." Galatians 4:4 says, "But at the right time, God sent His Son" (NLV). God is the true hero. God's kindness and His love appeared and saved us. When it seemed as though all hope was gone, Jesus, our Rescuer, showed up on the scene.

> God's kindness and grace is the beginning of our salvation, and it is grace that will keep us until the end.

The phrasing in Titus 3:5 actually makes me laugh, because God knows us so well. It says, "He saved us—not by works of righteousness that we had done, but according to his mercy." God knows our automatic tendency is to think, "Well, yeah, God is the one who saved me, but He did it because I try to be a good person." Nope. There's no room for that misconception. The notion that God saves us because of anything we do is undeniably false. He didn't save us because of our goodness or the "works of righteousness that we had done," but God saved us because of His mercy. He saved us because He is kind. He saved us because His heart has always been for us. God's kindness and grace is the beginning of our salvation, and it is grace that will keep us until the end.

God loves to shower us with His kindness. His kindness cannot be contained; it overflows out to His children. He is determined to bless us with His kindness for all of eternity. When we are assured that His heart for us is filled with kindness, we in turn are filled with love for Him. His kindness produces kindness in our hearts.

If today you feel like all hope is lost, if you feel like there isn't a hero to rescue you, or if you feel God's kindness has run out, remember our verse. God is for you, beloved. He is forever kind. He is forever full of love for you. If He didn't spare His own Son, how much more will He give you exactly what you need today?

GOODNESS

Questioning His Goodness

Give thanks to the LORD, for he is good;
his faithful love endures forever.

1 CHRONICLES 16:34

Like everyone, everywhere, I reached the end of 2020—and was glad it was over. What. A. Year. And I did not mean that in a good way. The year was difficult on a global level. The pandemic had taken millions of lives worldwide, with millions of people out of work and struggling financially because of the pandemic mitigation lockdown and restrictions, and attempted suicides and addictions skyrocketed with the strain to the psychological well-being of our world. At the same time, deep racial tension in our nation, with protests and true lament for injustice, were making its indelible mark on us. Political unrest was dividing friends and family in permanent ways. I reached the end of 2020, expecting some new terrible event to happen every week.

The year 2020 wasn't just difficult globally; it was difficult personally. I experienced loss in ways I never had before, with so much being stripped away from me—so many things I thought I needed, so many things that made me happy and gave me comfort. Without hesitation I can say 2020 was the hardest year of my life. In general I tend to be a look-on-the-bright-side type of person. But 2020 saw me shedding more tears than I'd cried in all the previous years.

I'm not alone in this. Friends and family repeated the same refrain: "2020 has been the hardest year of my life." It was a year for wondering about God's goodness. In 2020 I often wondered about God's goodness. Couldn't He see all the suffering? Didn't He care about the pain we were feeling? It actually felt as if God were piling on unnecessary heart-ache. Over and over I found myself praying out loud, "This is enough, God. We are hurting enough. Please make this stop."

The celebration of God's goodness, in our passage from Chronicles, stands in real contrast to these feelings—plainly endorsing God's goodness and His faithful love. And then I remember who it is that wrote this song of praise: David! David knew suffering. He understood what it was like to hide out in a cave while someone he loved chased him to try and kill him. He understood injustice. He understood what it was like to have his own sin cause terrible pain to so many people. He understood what it was like to feel far from God. And yet David is the one reminding himself and us who God really is: God is good. He is good at His very core. He literally cannot do wrong or evil. When things that we don't understand about God or the way He works makes us think He's bad, it actually means we don't see the bigger picture, we don't have the wisdom He does, and we don't truly understand what complete goodness is.

God is only ever good. This doesn't mean that noth-

The only thing that can redeem or repair brokenness is the goodness of God.

ing bad happens. Bad things happen all the time—with the whole year of 2020 as an excellent example. But bad things don't happen because God is bad; bad things happen because sin has broken everything. Sin has broken our relationship with God, our relationship with ourselves, our relationship with the world, and our relationship with each other. The only thing that can redeem or repair our brokenness is the goodness of God. His steadfast love endures forever.

In the middle of a bad day, or bad week, or bad year, or bad decade, remember our God. He is good. We experience that only in part now because of all the badness around us and in us, but one day we will experience His goodness fully and wholly, with everything we are. Until that day, we can work to bring God's kingdom here on earth by displaying God's goodness as much as we can and reveling in the fact that His goodness toward us will never end.

You Are Being Followed

Only goodness and faithful love will pursue me
all the days of my life,
and I will dwell in the house of the LORD
as long as I live.

PSALM 23:6 HCSB

I am not a fan of horror films. I actually have to close my eyes and put my fingers in my ears when a preview of one comes on at the movie theatre. I avoid scary and unsettling images because I am so susceptible to bad dreams. I still have nightmares from the movie *Gremlins* I saw when I was a kid. A couple Christmases ago we watched *Home Alone*, and I kid you not, I could not sleep because of dreaming that someone was trying to break into our house. So when I say that I am not a fan of horror films I mean it with the very core of who I am. Those scary movies often contain scenes where the main character is walking through a dark house, corn field, mall, or cemetery with the sense that someone is following them. The music builds and you see a close-up of their face, but what they don't know is you can also see someone lurking in the shadows waiting to attack. Gah! Did I mention I hate scary movies? I am creeping myself out.

A lot of us live our lives feeling as if something bad is following us. We remember a terrible thing we have done, and we are just waiting for payback. We are sure that at any second our just deserts will confront us, and we will have to face the consequences. Or maybe memories of something terrible that was done to us haunts us continually. We live with a sense of low-grade fear that at any second that bad thing will come back and get us again.

> **What if we looked for that goodness and faithful love throughout our day?**

The end of Psalm 23 speaks to something following us around, but it is not the shadowy darkness we dread. Goodness and faithful love pursue us. God doesn't just bless us once with the gift of salvation, but He pursues us with His blessings. He pursues us with His faithful love and with His goodness. He runs after us with all that He is. He doesn't just follow us with His goodness and steadfast love for the first few months of our salvation but rather He pursues us *all the days* of our lives. What would our lives look like if every day we woke up and thought, "His goodness and faithful love will pursue me today"? What if we looked for that goodness and faithful love throughout our day? How would our outlook on life be different if we were looking for His goodness instead of awaiting something terrible?

What does His goodness and faithful love look like in our lives? The New Living Translation takes Psalm 23 and delivers a beautiful rediscovery of this verse:

The LORD is my shepherd;
 I have all that I need.
He lets me rest in green meadows;
 he leads me beside peaceful streams.
 He renews my strength.
He guides me along right paths,
 bringing honor to his name.
Even when I walk
 through the darkest valley,
I will not be afraid,
 for you are close beside me.
Your rod and your staff
 protect and comfort me.
You prepare a feast for me
 in the presence of my enemies.
You honor me by anointing my head with oil.
 My cup overflows with blessings.
Surely your goodness and unfailing love will pursue me
 all the days of my life,
and I will live in the house of the LORD
 forever.

Look over your shoulder for His goodness today; I am sure you will find it is close at hand.

Just Can't Stop Talking About It

They will give a testimony of your great goodness
and will joyfully sing of your righteousness.
. . . The LORD is good to everyone;
his compassion rests on all he has made.

PSALM 145:7, 9

Have you had an experience you enjoyed so immensely you just couldn't stop talking about it? I have a good friend who is doing this with the TV series *The Chosen*. She takes every opportunity she gets to bring up watching that series. She has tried several tactics to get others of us to watch it. Finally, last night, under her direction, a few of us got together to start watching the series. Before two of the four episodes we watched, my friend raved that these

The proclaimers and the singers have seen the goodness of God. They bring that experience to its height by talking about it.

were her favorites. When we talked about getting together to watch the fifth episode, she exclaimed again, "Oh, that one is my favorite!" She really loves this show. Even the fact that we make fun of her over her love of the show doesn't dissuade her.

Something like this enthusiasm is what the psalmist is talking about when he says, "They will give a testimony of your great goodness and will joyfully sing of your righteousness." The proclaimers and the singers have seen the goodness of God. They have experienced it. They are bringing that experience to its height by talking about it. They can't help but share how good God is! They know He is good, and they want you to know too. Listen to the ways that God is described from Psalm 145:

His greatness is unsearchable.
His works are wondrous.
His acts are awe-inspiring.
He is highly praised.
His splendor and majesty are evident.
He is gracious and compassionate.
He is slow to anger.
He is great in faithful love.
He is good to everyone.
He is compassion to all He has made.
His kingdom is glorious and splendid.
He has done mighty acts.
He is faithful in all His words.
He is gracious in all His actions.
He helps those who fall.

He raises up the oppressed.
He gives us food.
He satisfies the desire of every living thing.
He is righteous and faithful.
He is near to those who call out to Him.
He guards those who love Him.
He destroys the wicked.

This psalm is an acrostic. It uses the letters of the Hebrew alphabet to prompt something wonderful about God. It might be a fun exercise to go through the alphabet and write a sentence of praise. Get creative with how you worship Him. He is good and worthy to be praised.

Protected by Goodness

The LORD is good,
a stronghold in a day of distress;
he cares for those who take refuge in him.

NAHUM 1:7

Have you ever wanted to do something good for someone but felt powerless to do anything meaningful? Sometimes I see a need and think, "I wish I had the money to give to that family to help," or "It would be so good if I knew the right thing to say in this moment," or "I feel so powerless to do the good that needs to be done." Other times I see a need and have no idea at all how to help. It's almost as if my brain stops working. Even worse, there are times when I see a need and the coldness and apathy that dwell in my heart take over, and I just ignore the need altogether.

Help cannot be truly given to someone in need or in distress unless the one giving the help has the means to help, the knowledge to help, and the desire to help. Nahum 1:7 beautifully reminds us that we have a God who has the power to help, the knowledge of how to help, and the goodness of character to help. God's goodness isn't ineffectual. His goodness moves Him to be good to us. The Hebrew word for *goodness* in this verse implies that actions taken because of this goodness are useful and helpful to the object of the goodness.

God has the means to demonstrate goodness toward us. In fact, Genesis 14:19 calls God the "Possessor of heaven and earth" (ESV). In Psalm 50:10–11 God says of Himself that "every animal of the forest is mine, the cattle on a thousand hills. I know every bird of the mountains, and the creatures of the field are mine." Acts 17:24–25 says, "The God who made the world and everything in it—he is Lord of heaven and earth—does not live in shrines made by hands. Neither is he served by human hands, as though he needed anything, since he himself gives everyone life and breath and all things." God lacks nothing. He owns all and supplies us with everything. His riches are incomparable.

Even in situations and times when you don't know what you need, God knows.

The Lord knows how to demonstrate His goodness toward us. He is a "stronghold in the day of distress." Do you ever feel completely weak and lost? He is your stronghold. He is your protector. You are not alone. You are not left unguarded. Even in situations and times when you don't know what you need or what would be best for you or your loved ones, God knows! He knows and is actively working for your good. His goodness compels Him to work for your good.

God's character is perfectly good, and that moves Him "to care for those who take refuge in Him." His power and knowledge are not detached from His goodness. He cares for you. His heart of love for you moves Him toward you. He doesn't just do good to you because it is the right thing to do. He does good to you and for you because His heart is full of care and love for you.

The following words were penned in 1865 by James Smith. Remember the goodness of God and take these words to heart.

> He careth for you. He thinks of you. He watches over you. He sympathizes with you. He feels the deepest interest in you. He ever seeks your welfare. He infallibly secures your good. Your misery touches his heart, your wants lie open to his view, and your cries enter into his ears.[1]

The Perfect Gift

Every good and perfect gift is from above, coming down from the Father of lights, who does not change like shifting shadows.

JAMES 1:17

Have you ever received a gift from someone and thought, "Do they know me at all?" I have received gifts from people who were close to me, and I thought, "They have no idea who I am or what I like." It is not a good feeling.

Some of you may be too young to remember but for a while there were shoes called Shape Ups that were supposed to give you a workout while you wore them. (Go ahead and Google them!) The bottom of the shoe was shaped with a hump in the middle. The thinking was that you had to work harder to walk as you wore them, resulting in some sort of exercise. The shoe was supposed to look like any other shoe, except it didn't—at all. One Christmas I asked for a pair of UGG boots. Now before you judge me, just know that my feet are almost always cold, and I was really hoping the boots would be a fix to that problem. I had only told one person I wanted these boots, and I was assured that they would procure the gift. When Christmas came and I opened the shoe-shaped box, I found that instead of my long anticipated UGGs there was a pair of boots that sort of look liked UGGs but were instead Shape Ups. And if you think UGGs are ugly, you should have seen these Frankenstein-esque shoes. This "gift" was less than "good or perfect" on a multitude of levels.

His gifts to us reveal His heart.

Putting aside how I responded to those boots (it wasn't pretty), let's consider James 1:17. What type of giver is our God? We know that every "good and perfect gift" comes from His heart to you. He gives to us out of the goodness of who He is. His gifts to us reveal His heart. He is all goodness and no evil. His gifts to us are meant to showcase the utter goodness of who He is.

God's gifts aren't just good, they are perfect. Every gift He gives is perfectly suited for the one receiving the gift. He is keenly aware of everything you need. You are loved by a Father who not only is good but who also knows you more intimately than any other person. He is genuinely concerned about your well-being and cares for your soul in the most personal way. He knows what you need, and His goodness compels Him to give it to you. He longs to take care of you. His goodness makes Him generous.

The end of our verse reassures us that God will never change. He is the "Father of lights, who does not change like shifting shadows." He isn't going to trick you with a pair of

Shape Ups that sort of look like the shoes you wanted but aren't really them at all. He is all light and no shadow. He is all truth and no tricks. He is not about the "bait and switch." He promises goodness and will fulfill His promise.

How has our Father been good to us? He brings us into His family and calls Himself our Father. He will never withhold something good from you without giving you Himself instead. He gives the gift of faith to our unbelieving and doubting hearts. He gives forgiveness to you and me for every single sin we have committed in the past and will commit in the future. He makes you His own and commits to taking care of you. So today look around for the gifts all around you. Pray that your eyes are opened to the goodness and the perfectness of the gifts, and let those gifts turn your heart to praise to the Father of Lights.

FAITHFULNESS

Faithful to the End

*Know that the LORD your God is God, the faithful God who keeps
his gracious covenant loyalty for a thousand generations with those
who love him and keep his commands.*

DEUTERONOMY 7:9

During the pandemic, I heard about a couple named Sher-
wood and Doris Pope. They had been married sixty-one years
when they contracted COVID-19 around Thanksgiving of
2020. After a few weeks in the hospital, they lost their battle
with the virus and died only minutes apart, while holding
hands. Their son Shelton said this about them, "She loved
that man, and he loved her."[1] I love stories about couples who
were faithful all the way through their marriages, until—as
they promised in their vows—death parted them. Stories of
love and faithfulness make us stop and pay attention because
they speak to a longing deep inside of us. They make us ache
to experience forever-faithfulness.

Deuteronomy 7:9 declares that God will keep His promises
to His people. He is "the faithful God"—faithfulness is who He

is in His essence. In the great love stories we read or the couples whose married lives inspire us, we see character attributes that drew the partners together and something lovely and compelling that keeps the love light burning. In the case of God's love for us, it's not our charming character that draws Him but His essential faithfulness and choosing that leads to lasting fidelity.

Backing up a few verses to Deuteronomy 7:7–8, we find the reason why God decided to be faithful to His people: "The LORD had his heart set on you and chose you, not because you were more numerous than all peoples, for you were the fewest of all peoples. But because the LORD loved you and kept the oath he swore to your ancestors, he brought you out with a strong hand and redeemed you from the place of slavery, from the power of Pharaoh king of Egypt." The Lord doesn't "set His heart on" or "choose" His people because they are great or amazing or because somehow they will make Him look good. The Lord loves us and keeps His oath to us because that is who He is! He is loving and faithful to His people. His love is what makes us lovable. This is good news because if His faithfulness was based on anything we did, we would be in real trouble. We fail, we are inconsistent, and our love for Him ebbs and flows. Because His faithfulness is not based on our goodness, we can know with certainty

Our longing for faithful love is fulfilled in the character of our God.

that His covenant to take care of us, love us, and be our God will never be broken. We can rest assured of His unending promise to us.

So the next time you hear a heartrending love story, remember that the longing for faithful love is fulfilled in the character of our God. He is faithful. He keeps His covenant loyalty. He has set His love upon you, and nothing can make Him change His mind. That type of faithfulness should move your heart to love Him back. That type of faithfulness makes me desire to be faithful to Him. And here is the really mind-blowing truth: even on the days when you are unfaithful and forget about Him, His promises remain the same.

Common Temptation, Uncommon Faithfulness

No temptation has come upon you except what is common to humanity. But God is faithful; he will not allow you to be tempted beyond what you are able, but with the temptation he will also provide the way out so that you may be able to bear it.

1 CORINTHIANS 10:13

Have you ever felt like the things you struggle with, the temptations you feel, must be worse than the temptations that other people face? One time, when I was a mom of little ones, I was sitting in a small group listening to a friend talk about how she felt horrible because she hadn't read her Bible in two days, and that she felt far from God. In that moment, I realized I didn't even know how long it had been since I had read my Bible. My friend was grieved, and I wondered when I had ever felt really grieved over not reading my Bible. I felt horribly convicted then because I had also yelled at my kids and said horrible things—and I barely even cared that I had. Loneliness and anger had become the controlling influences in my life. I froze in my seat, hearing those around me agree with how hard it was when it had only been a couple days without praying or a devotional time. I wondered if everyone in the room could tell what a hard-hearted fraud I was since I wasn't jumping in to tell about my own experience. I was sure I was the worst person in the room. I couldn't believe that any single one of them had ever felt the things I felt or thought the same thoughts that I had. I am not at all trying to belittle my friend's true experience of heartbreak over her neglect of Bible reading. She was genuinely surprised that anyone in the group related to her. She came in feeling like the worst sinner in the group, but when she heard that others also struggled with their devotional time, she was encouraged that she wasn't alone. Maybe if I had spoken up about my own struggles, I'd have walked away encouraged as well. But shame keeps us hidden, in the dark, alone, feeling like the absolute worst, and unable to be honest.

But the beginning of 1 Corinthians 10:13 calls our temptations "common to humanity." Eugene Peterson paraphrased is this way: "No test or temptation that comes your way is

God's faithfulness binds Him to us in the midst of our unfaithfulness.

beyond the course of what others have had to face" (MSG). You are not alone. Others have faced whatever temptation you have faced.

Others who have gone before you have walked the test that you are walking. While this knowledge brings a level of comfort; there is more solace to come in this verse.

God is faithful! Despite our wandering hearts and wandering actions, you and I have a God who remains faithful and committed to keeping us. His faithfulness is active. His faithfulness is effective. His faithfulness isn't just a nice sentiment with no power behind it. His faithfulness binds Him to us in the midst of our unfaithfulness. When the verse says, "He will not allow you to be tempted beyond what you are able," that means we can go through anything with Him—because He can handle anything. We obviously don't have the strength to withstand temptation alone, but because we are not alone, He gives us the ability to say "no" when we are tempted by whatever is contrary to His will for our lives. He promises to be with us and to provide a way for us to escape the temptation we feel.

Now you might be thinking, "That's great in theory, but I give in to temptation all the time. I don't take His help. I don't take the way of escape. So now what?" Let me lead you to another verse that talks about God's faithfulness. First John 1:9 says this: "If we confess our sins, he is faithful and righteous to forgive us our sins and to cleanse us from all unrighteousness." Our gracious heavenly Father promises to be faithful even when we fail. He promises to forgive us when we give in to temptation. This should give you the courage to try yet again to withstand temptation. Don't let shame have the last word. Grace gets the last word. God's faithfulness gets the last word. We can resist and rest in that today.

The Seesaw

But the Lord is faithful; he will strengthen you
and guard you from the evil one.

2 THESSALONIANS 3:3

My heart is a perpetual seesaw. One day I am all in, committed to the Lord, zealous for His glory, devoted to His kingdom. On those days I am overjoyed that I get to read His words to me and that I am able to talk to Him; I am sure He is near me and listening. The next day thoughts of God don't even enter my mind, or when they do, I quickly shoo them away, refocusing on myself. On those days I don't pray, I don't read my Bible, and I don't even care that I don't. Some days my fickle heart swings back and forth between those two extremes, hot and cold, up

> While I'm on my perpetual seesaw, God isn't up one day and down the next.

and down, several times a day. Lots and lots of days, I am somewhere in the apathetic middle. Maybe you can relate.

Whatever my circumstances, whatever my mood, whatever my attention span, what I need more than anything on all of these days is to be convinced that "the Lord is faithful." He never wavers. While I'm on my perpetual seesaw, God isn't up one day and down the next. His affections for me are always steady.

John MacDuff, a nineteenth-century Scottish pastor, wrote this:

> How comforting to you amid the ebbings and flowings of your changing history, to know that the change is all with you, and not with your God! Your spiritual vessel may be tossed on waves of temptation, in many a dark midnight. You may think your pilot has left you, and be ready continually to say, "Where is my God?" But fear not! The ship which bears your spiritual destiny is in better hands than yours; a golden chain of covenant love links it to the eternal throne! That chain can never snap asunder. He who holds it in His hand gives you this as the pledge of your safety—"Because I live, you shall live also."[2]

Dear friend, the change is always with us; it is never with our Father. Because He is so true in His character, He continues to be faithful to us.

God's faithfulness guarantees that He will strengthen us. On those days, weeks, months, or maybe even years when you feel weak, as if you will not make it to the end of your race, you can know that He promises to give you strength. He will not lie to you. He has promised to strengthen you, and God will never fail to keep His promises.

God's faithfulness to us also guarantees that He will guard us from the evil one. There are days when I feel unguarded, days when I feel the temptation is too much, and days when I actually give in to living in opposition to what I know God wants from me. Even on those days God is guarding me. His protective hand over my life claims that I am His and He is mine. He will not let the evil one have me. God will by His strength and His faithfulness keep me by His side and in His family.

God is utterly dependable. There is not one single second of one single day when He forgets to guard us or to strengthen us or to keep us. His heart remains always dedicated to His children. His heart is unendingly faithful toward you and me, even on the days where we are utterly unfaithful to Him. His love for us and His heart for us will never allow Him to be anything but faithful from now until eternity.

The Promise

Let us hold on to the confession of our hope without wavering,
since he who promised is faithful.

HEBREWS 10:23

Two of my kids sat me down in front of a computer and told me that they needed me to watch something. I was nervous, to say the least. Honestly, I feel like I never know what is coming. Was this going to be a funny video, or a boring Minecraft stream, or something they thought was hilarious but I wouldn't understand at all? I had no idea. But then they opened up Google Slides; I was intrigued. My oldest cleared his throat and said, "We have a presentation for you." I looked at the first slide and saw "List of Reasons to Get Another Dog." What followed was a series of slides with a multitude of promises. "We will feed the dog. We will take the dog on walks. We will clean up after the dog. We will. We will. We will." On and on the list went. After the promises, the kids included slides about available animal rescues in our area. The two of them had thought through every one of my objections and dismantled them all.

Truth be told, I couldn't resist. We got the dog. Let me just say, I love this dog. I cannot imagine our lives without him and his terrible breath. But as for that list of promises . . . I am sure you can guess what happened. The children hung in there, true to their oaths, for about a month before I became the primary caretaker of the doggo.

While I want to come down hard on my kids for not keeping their promises, I am all too familiar with the fact that I also fail to do a myriad of things that I know I should. This is part of the Christian life. The more I know of God, the more I see I am unlike Him. The thing I am consistent at is falling short of what brings glory to God, and the thing that He is consistent at is forgiving me and bringing me back home.

Hebrews 10:23 encourages Christ followers to hold on to our "confession of hope without wavering." Initially, that seems like one more promise we need to try to keep—and potentially one more promise we will break. If we are honest with ourselves, holding on to hope "without wavering" seems impossible, because we know we are unfaithful, we know we waver. But the next part of the verse comes to the rescue. At first glance the back half of the verse doesn't seem to go with front half. It goes on to say, "Since he who promised is faithful."

We can hold on without wavering because He is holding on to us.

In other words, the Scripture is telling you, "Hold on without wavering because He has you." The promise that is being referred to is the promise of forgiveness. The whole of Hebrews 10 talks about the faithfulness of Jesus, our High Priest, to forgive our sins. He is faithful to forgive an unfaithful people. Because of His faithfulness we can hold on without wavering because He is holding on to us. He is the Faithful One.

Today when you encounter a promise you have broken or the broken promises of friends and family, you can remember that there is One who is always faithful. He is faithful to forgive. He is faithful to love. He is faithful to keep you.

The Rider

Then I saw heaven opened, and there was a white horse.
Its rider is called Faithful and True.

REVELATION 19:11

I love the book of Revelation. The book is sort of like that weird uncle you don't spend much time with but when you do you think, "Wow. He is actually really cool—in a strange way." Our verse for today comes right in the middle of an epic worship service—a worship service that will one day show us what worship is meant to be. There will be no divided heart, no sin to hinder, no distractedness, just everyone giving up their Hallelujah to Jesus: "Then I heard something like the voice of a vast multitude, like the sound of cascading waters, and like the rumbling of loud thunder, saying, 'Hallelujah, because our Lord God, the Almighty, reigns! Let us be glad, rejoice, and give him glory, because the marriage of the Lamb has come, and his bride has prepared herself. She was given fine linen to wear, bright and pure'" (Rev. 19:6–8). God in and of Himself is enough for us to worship for a lifetime, but these verses offer

The Lord dresses us in every faithful and good work Jesus performed here on earth. God brings us into His happiness.

a glimpse of yet another reason why we should "be glad, rejoice, and give Him glory." We get to marry our King! The church—that is, you and I—is part of this celebration because we are the bride of Christ. He has prepared us for Himself and has given us "fine linen to wear, bright and pure." He took our dirty robes, tattered by our sin and by the world, and He "washed their robes and made them white in the blood of the Lamb" (Rev. 7:14). The Lord dresses us in every faithful and good work Jesus performed here on earth. God brings us into His happiness.

Charles Spurgeon talked about this marriage feast:

Beloved, the marriage supper is a feast of love; there, love is at home. So Jesus, that he may reveal himself in his love best of all, appears as a bleeding sacrifice on the day of his love's triumph. I do not know how to talk about this great theme; but this truth rests in my heart, and makes me feel more glad than I can tell. It lies like a cake of sweet perfume upon the altar of my soul, and burns there with the soft lambent flame of love; and I rejoice to know that, in the day when Jesus takes his Church by the hand, and leads her home to his Father's house, he will appear in that character in which he most of all has shown his love to his beloved. You see most of his love when you see most of his griefs, and most of his condescension; and therefore in that character does he appear at his marriage supper."[3]

The verse we're focusing on today refers to Jesus on a white horse, and "the rider is called Faithful and True." That Rider is our Savior, the one who loved us unto death, the One who left complete bliss to come to earth to serve, to give, and to lay His life down so we could be married to Him forever. We can take part in the marriage supper of the Lamb. The Lamb who takes away the sin of the world binds Himself to us in a sacramental covenant. His word to us is Faithful and True. His character toward us is Faithful and True. His promises to us are Faithful and True. We will be His forever.

There isn't much in this life you can count on wholly. But, dear ones, we have our Jesus, and He is Faithful and True.

GENTLENESS

The Gentle Whisper

After the earthquake came a fire, but the LORD was not in the fire.
And after the fire came a gentle whisper.

1 KINGS 19:12 NIV

I once was part of a small group when the getting-to-know-each-other, icebreaker question posed to the group was, "What animal best describes you?" Another time, group members were asked to give three words to describe ourselves. For sure, these icebreakers put you on the spot. You have to quickly figure out how to present yourself, curating the image you want to project in that group. Truth be told, there are days, and lots of them, when the three words to describe me would be *annoyed, disinterested,* and *bored*—and, let's be honest, no one wants that much authenticity! To really get to know someone, you have to ask questions, all kinds. You find out what they like and dislike, you find out about vocation and hobbies and families. You ask others to show you what they are all about.

Today's passage from 1 Kings describes a time when God showed Elijah what He was all about. Elijah, a prophet whose story appears in the Old Testament, was depressed—genuinely depressed and not just a little sad. He was depressed about the way everything was going, and he had good reason to be. From his circumstances, it seemed as if God had abandoned him. Eugene Peterson paraphrased the story this way:

> When Elijah saw how things were, he ran for dear life to Beersheba, far in the south of Judah. He left his young servant there and then went on into the desert another day's journey. He came to a lone broom bush and collapsed in its shade, wanting in the worst way to be done with it all—to just die: "Enough of this, GOD! Take my life—I'm ready to join my ancestors in the grave!" Exhausted, he fell asleep under the lone broom bush. (1 Kings 19:3–5 MSG)

Elijah begs God to take his life. He is done. Then an angel comes and gives him some food, and Elijah takes a nap. It is amazing how often a meal and nap help. Then Elijah sleeps and eats again, and then he sets out toward the mountain of God. There he has a conversation with the "word of the LORD." He is asked, "What are you doing here, Elijah?" and Elijah basically responds with, "I have done everything I am supposed to do, and all of Your people are a bunch of screw-ups. I am the only one left who is doing things right and loves you." Then God tells Elijah that He is going to show Himself to him.

This, my friends, is where it gets really interesting. God indulges Elijah and us—far better than any icebreaker game. He shows Elijah who He is and reveals exactly what He wants to be known by: "A hurricane wind ripped through the mountains and shattered the rocks before GOD, but GOD wasn't to be found in the wind; after the wind an earthquake, but GOD wasn't in the earthquake; and after the earthquake fire, but GOD wasn't in the fire" (MSG). Get the picture? These extraordinary, power-

God often comes in the ways we least expect.

ful events occur—events you would expect God to use to reveal Himself, especially to someone who is doubting His power, someone who thinks he is all alone with no one to fight for him. But God doesn't work the way we work. Instead God chooses to reveal who He is in a "gentle whisper" (NIV).

Who is this God who reveals Himself through quietness and gentleness versus strength and might? God is all-powerful and mighty, which is why His choice to show us this gentle side of Him is even more mind-blowing. God often comes in the ways we least expect. He comes in the gentle whisper. He comes with food and instructions to sleep. He is gentle with us; it is who He is. Our God who delights to reveal Himself in a "gentle whisper" is with you today. Look for Him. He might show up in the most unforeseen ways.

Gentleness
Makes Us Great

You have also given me the shield of Your salvation,
and Your right hand upholds me;
and Your gentleness makes me great.

PSALM 18:35 NASB

It might be easier for us to see Jesus as gentle than it is for us to see God the Father as gentle. Gentleness may not be our first thought about any part of the triune God when we're focusing on ourselves and worrying about what God thinks of us. Then we tend to think of the Father as wrathful, vengeful, and angry. Yet again God comes to us through His Word to correct our faulty thinking. To a certain extent we know ourselves. We know that we don't live up to the standard God asks of us. We know we don't love the way we should. We aren't gentle like we should be. We aren't kind like we should be. We don't care for others' needs like we should. We're disappointed with ourselves, and so we expect Him to be disappointed and angry

We are saved from God by God for God.

with us. Yet God isn't like us. He doesn't hold grudges, and He isn't harsh with us. The wrath of God the Father toward our sin was poured out on Jesus while He hung on Calvary's tree. So now there is no wrath left for His beloved children, but only grace, love, acceptance, and forgiveness.

God shields us with His salvation. We are saved from God by God for God. We are protected by the God of the universe. He is our salvation. He is our shield. That doesn't mean that difficulties and hardships will not come crashing into our lives, but it does mean we can know without any doubt that He is with us in those sufferings. He has saved us from the one thing that really would cause our utter destruction—an eternity without Him. He also saves us from what we think of ourselves and what others think of us. He proclaims over our lives that we are His beloved children. He has saved us to be a part of His family.

God's right hand upholds us. In the Old Testament, the portion of the Scriptures where you can find the book of Psalms, the right hand of God is a symbol for a place of great honor. Not only does God save us, but He puts us in a place of honor. He supports and upholds us there. He cares for us there. His kindness is beyond what we can imagine. His heart of love toward us is pure and whole. There is no part of God that holds something against us. The Father honors us because He honors the Son, and we are hidden in the Son.

God's gentleness makes us great. The way He loves us, the way He honors us, the way He protects us, the way He shields us, reveals His heart. His character is what makes us great. This is why we look at who He is. This is one of the benefits of studying and reveling in how gentle God is. The more we see that He is gentle, the more we long to be close to Him and become like Him. If we think of God as One who is harsh we will want to avoid Him, but if we see Him as the gentle, kind Father that He is we will run to Him.

Today remember that you are shielded, you are saved, you are upheld, you are honored by our Father. Pray that the Holy Spirit reminds you of His gentleness toward you, and let His gentleness make you great.

The Shepherd

He tends his flock like a shepherd:
He gathers the lambs in his arms
and carries them close to his heart;
he gently leads those that have young.

ISAIAH 40:11 NIV

During an ultrasound for my pregnancy with my youngest child, the technician stopped what he was doing and stepped away. He was gone for what felt like a year before returning with another technician, who with no explanation promptly went about performing the job that had been left unfinished. They stood and looked at the machine, I strained to see what they were looking at. Of course, I had no idea, but I could tell whatever "it" was, "it" wasn't good. Finally, the second tech looked at me and said, "We can only find three chambers of the heart. That doesn't necessarily mean the fourth chamber isn't there; it just means we can't see it. You will need to come back in a month so we can look at this again. We hope to be able to get a better picture." With that he handed me a tissue to wipe the gel off my stomach and left. I lay there, confused, scared, and disbelieving. What had just happened? What did this mean for my baby? A myriad of questions swirled in my mind as I drove home. I stopped at the mailbox at the bottom of our driveway, reached in, and pulled out the mail. There was a card from a friend, congratulating me on the pregnancy. The verse on the card is the one we're focusing on today. I read the verse, and I wept. Our sweet Savior was assuring me that He was my good shepherd.

The Good Shepherd is doing the same for you today. Who is this God who promises to carry those who can't walk on their own? Who is this God who brings us close to His heart? Who is this God who gently leads us because He knows we are weak and feeble and in need of extra tenderness? He is our God.

Somehow, we've got our ideas twisted. We think of God as one who demands the impossible from us and then doles out angry discipline when we do not come through. We hear Him say we must be holy as He is holy, and we wonder how that is even possible. I cannot even make it an hour without finding my heart longing for something other than what He gives. We don't think of the Lord as a tender shepherd but rather as a harsh taskmaster just waiting for us to screw up so that He can disappointedly shake His head at us and then begrudgingly forgive us because He promised to. But no! That is not the picture given in Isaiah

God does ask the impossible, but then He accomplishes the impossible for us.

40:11. God does ask the impossible, but then He accomplishes the impossible for us. He tends to us. He cares for us. He gathers us. He carries us. He keeps us. He is gentle because He knows we are as helpless as little lambs.

Beloved, you do not have a God who is disinterested in your pain. You do not have a Shepherd who looks at the mess you are in and says, "This is your fault. Get yourself out of this." You do not have a Father who rejects you. You have a God who holds you close. You have a Shepherd who understands every weakness that troubles your heart. You have a Father who accepts you because you are wrapped in Christ.

Oh, that the gentleness of God would change how we interact with others today, that His tenderness with you and me would break our hearts and persuade us to be gentle with those around us. See your Shepherd, see your God, see your Father gently holding you, no matter what today holds.

Come

I am gentle and humble in heart.

MATTHEW 11:29 NIV

This self-description of Jesus comes in one of my favorite passages of the Bible. You are probably familiar with it, but please take the time to read it now: "Come to me, all you who are weary and burdened, and I will give you rest. Take my yoke upon you and learn from me, for I am gentle and humble in heart, and you will find rest for your souls. For my yoke is easy and my burden is light" (Matt. 11:28–30 NIV). Our sweet Savior is offering a correction to our perception of Him.

Often when I am weary and burdened, I wonder how I got in that spot. I wonder why I am in such a funk. Typically, that spirals into thinking about all the ways I have ignored my God and the needs of my soul. I start listing off all of my failures: *spent too much time on social media, didn't read my Bible, haven't prayed*

Jesus calls us away from ourselves. Jesus calls us to Himself.

in who knows how long, wasn't really listening to the sermon at church, ignored the thought that I should reach out to a friend I know is hurting, etc. I end up wallowing in self-criticism until I feel even more weary and burdened, which usually ends with me sitting down with a bag of pita chips munching until I am sufficiently distracted. I go to myself for relief from myself. And I can say with complete confidence that this strategy absolutely does not ever work.

Jesus calls us away from ourselves. Jesus calls us to Himself: "Come to me." Eugene Peterson puts the invitation from Jesus this way: "Come to me. Get away with me, and you'll recover your life" (MSG). When we are weary and burdened because of our sin or just from the hardships of life, Jesus calls us to come back to Him. He does not await our return with a wooden spoon to administer discipline with a scowling face, or even with a disappointed look. He knows we need to hear about who He is in order to draw us back to Him.

Jesus says, "I am gentle and humble in heart." He isn't demanding exact judgment or even making sure we know all we have done wrong. He is there, promising rest; He actually promises it twice in these verses. He is there, asking us to learn from Him. Jesus isn't at all what we are used to in this world. We expect to get what we deserve—harshness, or a slap on the hand because we haven't kept up our end of some bargain.

Our gentle Jesus rejects any bargaining with Him. He will not accept your good works as a way back to get into His good graces. He reminds you of His character instead of demanding that you change yours. He is gentle. He is gentle with every hurt in your life. He is gentle with you every time you realize you have inadvertently been carried away, and He is gentle with you every time you rebelliously seek after anything except what He is offering to you. He is gentle with your missteps and mistakes, and all the while He is wooing you back to Himself. He desires to teach you this part of His heart. He isn't harsh, domineering, or rough, even when you expect Him to be, even when He has a right to be.

So friends, hear the call today from your Savior: "Are you tired? Worn out? Burned out on religion? Come to me. Get away with me and you'll recover your life. I'll show you how to take a real rest. Walk with me and work with me—watch how I do it. Learn the unforced rhythms of grace. I won't lay anything heavy or ill-fitting on you. Keep company with me and you'll learn to live freely and lightly" (Matt. 11:28–30 MSG).

Unexpected
Gentleness

Tell Daughter Zion, "See, your King is coming to you, gentle,
and mounted on a donkey, and on a colt, the foal of a donkey."

This verse appears first in Zechariah 9:9 and then again here in Matthew. Let me give you little bit of context to make the gentleness of our King even more devastatingly powerful for you. Jesus had asked His disciples to find a donkey for Him so He could fulfill the prophecy from Zechariah. This takes place right before Jesus' triumphal entry into Jerusalem on what we call Palm Sunday. This was at the climax of His ministry, when He was most popular. He had been healing the sick, restoring sight to the blind, raising Lazarus from the dead, and now is coming into Jerusalem for the final act in His life.

The disciples and His followers are expecting Jesus to come into Jerusalem to take power, to overthrow the Romans, and to set things right for the Jewish people. Yet Jesus does the unexpected. He asks the disciples to go find Him a donkey, a lowly animal and not, surely, an animal fit for a King about to take political power from those in control. What would have been expected is for the King to come into battle on a horse, but this isn't who Jesus was then and it isn't who He is now. He is described as gentle.

Jesus was poor. He became poor for us, in every respect. He didn't even have His own donkey. He had to ask to borrow one. Our King was not ashamed of His need. He did not just have compassion for the poor and offer platitudes about caring for those who have less than others, He became one of us. I have heard it said that compassion is less about what we do to serve the needy and more about us choosing to see ourselves as needy too. This is what Jesus did for us. He chose to become human. He became poor. He became needy.

This One, the One whom the fullness of God dwells in, had to borrow a donkey!

The One who had to borrow a donkey is the same One described in Colossians 1:

In him all things were created: things in heaven and on earth, visible and invisible, whether thrones or powers or rulers or authorities; all things have been created through him and for him. He is before all things, and in him all things hold together. And he is the head of the body, the church; he is the beginning and the firstborn from among the dead, so that in everything he might have the supremacy. For God was pleased to have all his fullness dwell in him. (Col. 1:16–19 NIV)

This One, the One whom the fullness of God dwells in, had to borrow a donkey! He did all this so we would know Him as a King riding in on a donkey, coming not to be served, "but to serve, and to give his life as a ransom for many" (Matt. 20:28).

Jesus did this so when we see our King we believe it when He says He is "gentle and humble in heart." We see Him "humble and riding on a donkey." Martin Luther described this scene: "Here there is no violence, no armor, no power, no anger, no wrath. . . . Here there are only kindness, justice, salvation, mercy, and every good thing."[1]

Jesus' entry declares, "I am meek, lowly, humble. I am approachable." He wants you to come to Him. He wants you to see Him as your majestic King, but not the type of King we are familiar with. He is a King who identifies with you. He is a King who rode into Jerusalem that day for you. He is a King who refuses to make being rich and powerful His identity. Instead, He chooses the word *gentle*. Daughter of Zion, see your King today. He is coming to you.

Acknowledgments

Thank you to the community at RISEN church for being a place of healing, a place of joy, a place of encouragement, a place of restoration, a place of rest, and a place of safety for me. Especially to those on staff: Martin and Angela Cachero, Kirsten Loy (Lady Risen, Mamarito), Travis Augustine (E-Mallow, Willis), Caitlyn Gajo, Irina Darrow, Nichole Mays, and Lowercase jess, you all have supported me and cheered me on, and I love you guys. I love our Tuesday mornings. You have taught me more than you know.

To my family: I couldn't have made it through the last year without your love, support, laughter, and encouragement. God has used you all to be the light at the end of this dark tunnel. I am not using hyperbole; I really do not know where I would be without you.

Trillia Newbell, thank you for believing I still had something valuable to say when I really thought my writing career was over. I am grateful.

Notes

Love

1. John Ross Macduff, *The Morning Watches and Night Watches* (London: J. Nisbet, 1853), 43–44.
2. Charles Spurgeon, sermon "Deep Calleth unto Deep," April 1869, The Spurgeon Center, accessed June 8, 2021, https://www.spurgeon .org/resource-library/sermons/deep-calleth-unto-deep/#flipbook/.
3. Charles Spurgeon, sermon "Immeasurable Love," July 1885, The Spurgeon Center, https://www.spurgeon.org/resource-library/ sermons/immeasurable-love/#flipbook/.
4. John Flavel, "Oh what a melting consideration is this," Grace Gems, accessed June 8, 2021, https://www.gracegems.org/2018/01/O%20 what%20a%20melting%20consideration%20is%20this.html.
5. Michael Reeves, *Delighting in the Trinity: An Introduction to the Christian Faith* (Downers Grove, IL: InterVarsity Press, 2012), 76.

Joy

1. John Calvin and William Pringle, *Commentary on the Book of the Prophet Isaiah, vol. 4* (Bellingham, WA: Logos Bible Software, 2010), 399–400, app.logos.com.
2. J. C. Ryle, *Commentary on the Book of Luke*, Grace Gems, accessed June 17, 2021, https://www.gracegems.org/Ryle/l15.htm.

3. Dante Stuart, "Revisiting the Theology of the Negro Spiritual," June 28, 2017, *The Witness*, https://thewitnessbcc.com/revisiting-theology-negro-spiritual/.

Peace

1. Octavius Winslow, "Emmanuel, or Titles of Christ," 1869, Grace Gems, accessed June 17, 2021, https://www.gracegems.org/W/e6.htm.
2. G. Walter Hansen, *The Letter to the Philippians*, The Pillar New Testament Commentary (Grand Rapids, MI: Eerdmans, 2009), 292.

Patience

1. Chad Bird, *Unveiling Mercy: 365 Daily Devotions Based on Insights from Old Testament Hebrew* (Irvine, CA: 1517 Publishing, 2020), 122.
2. J. A. Simpson and E. S. C. Weiner, *The Oxford English Dictionary* (Oxford: Clarendon Press, 1989).

Kindness

1. James Smith, *Treasures from James Smith 1802-1862,* Grace Gems, https://gracegems.org/D/smith.htm.
2. Dane C. Ortlund, *Gentle and Lowly: The Heart of Christ for Sinners and Sufferers* (Wheaton, IL: Crossway Books, 2020), 151.

Goodness

1. James Smith, *Bright Rays and Reviving Showers; or, A Book for All Characters and All Times* (London: T. Nelson and Sons, 1865), 7.

Faithfulness

1. Amy Cutler and Nexstar Media Wire, "North Carolina Couple Married for 61 Years Dies of COVID-19 Minutes Apart, Holding Hands," FOX 46 Charlotte, December 20, 2020,

https://www.fox46.com/news/north-carolina-couple-married-for-61-years-dies-of-covid-19-minutes-apart-holding-hands-2/.

2. John MacDuff, "The Faithful Promiser," 1849, Grace Gems, https://gracegems.org/book4/MacDuff_Promiser.htm.

3. Charles Spurgeon, "The Marriage Supper of the Lamb," August 21, 1887, The Spurgeon Center, https://www.spurgeon.org/resource-library/sermons/the-marriage-supper-of-the-lamb/#flipbook/.

Gentleness

1. Martin Luther, quoted in Edward A. Engelbreit, *The Lutheran Study Bible* (St. Louis, MO: Concordia Publishing House, 2009), 1535.

Front Porch with the Fitzes is a weekly chinwag featuring author Elyse Fitzpatrick, her husband, affectionately known as Pop, and two of her three kids, Jessica Thompson and Joel Fitzpatrick. Sometimes some unexpected folks might even drop by and sit for a spell. Every week they'll jibber about family life, things that interest them in culture or news, and what they're learning about the Lord. Imagine sitting on the front porch of your ol' Kentucky home, listening to three slightly off-kilter believers talk about life, do a lot of laughing at each other and everyone else . . . and then, of course, there's always the bluegrass music playing in the background.